Arguments

Series editor: John Harrison

'As we plunge deeper into the crisis caused by monetarism and militarism, more and more people will be turning to socialist ideas to find out more about socialism and what socialists are saying.

Arguments for Socialism is developing as an essential reading list for the interested as well as the committed and offers a compact library of essential background information and clear analysis.' *Tony Benn*

Other **Arguments for Socialism**

Hidden Hands

Women and Economic Policies

Anne Phillips

Pluto Press

First published in 1983 by Pluto Press Limited,
The Works, 105a Torriano Avenue,
London NW5 2RX

British Library Cataloguing in Publication Data
Phillips, Anne
Hidden hands.—(Arguments for socialism)
1. Women—Economic conditions
I. Title
330.9'0088042   HQ1381
ISBN 0-86104-511-4

Cover designed by Clive Challis A Gr R
Computerset by Promenade Graphics Limited
Block 23a Lansdown Industrial Estate, Cheltenham GL51 8PL
Printed and bound in Great Britain
by Richard Clay (The Chaucer Press) Limited, Bungay, Suffolk

Contents

Acknowledgements

In writing this book I have drawn extensively on discussions in the 'Sex and Class' group of the Conference of Socialist Economists, and I am particularly grateful to the members of the London group for all those pleasant evenings. Special thanks to people who read and commented on early drafts: Cynthia Cockburn, Jenny Earle, Trevor Evans, Sue Himmelweit, Jenny Hurstfield, Eileen Phillips, and Barbara Taylor. New Ways to Work and the Low Pay Unit were generous with their time and information, but neither should be held responsible for any errors. John Harrison and Richard Kuper gave useful editorial advice, and Ciaran Driver acted throughout in the difficult role of male economist, alternately encouraging me to be more utopian or more down to earth. The ideas are not so much mine but those of many socialist feminists; I hope I have set them out clearly.

Introduction

Economics has never had much to say about women. When we think of the great economic issues of the day we think of questions like: How do we create full employment? Can we rescue manufacturing industry in Britain? Should we nationalise the banks? We rarely think of these as relating to women. Some vigilant feminist might break in here, asking what full employment means for women, or why manufacturing is three-quarters men? She will probably be ticked off for missing the point and redirected to the women's committee. Women's questions are dealt with under a separate item – dismissed to the limbo of social policy, away from the heat of economic debate.

None of this is surprising. Economics is very much a male pursuit and the makers of economic policy are overwhelmingly male. When women reach positions of power in national or local government they usually find themselves looking after education, health or consumer affairs – on the 'softer' edge of policy-making. They are rarely prominent in matters of finance, employment or planning.

The same pattern repeats itself inside the labour movement, where debates on economic strategy have been largely debates between men. In 1982 the TUC and Labour Party produced a joint document on *Economic Planning and Industrial Democracy*: the committee which prepared it was made up of 31 men and 2 women. In the same year the Labour Party produced a report on *The City*: the study group responsible contained 34 men and only 1 woman. Women might have something useful to say on education, but the economic issues of the day will be decided by men.

Some of this stems from the way we define the economy. The activities that can dominate women's lives – looking after children, caring for sick relatives, shopping, cleaning, washing, cooking – none of these will figure in the 'economy'. Under capitalism we only really count things when money changes hands. So official statistics for the economically active exclude housewives, and measures of the nation's output ignore their work. Much of what women are supposed to do with their time has been defined out of the economy.

But even when women go out to work they carry on being invisible. Since the 1950s there has been a startling increase in women's wage employment – having stayed at 30 per cent of the labour force for decades, they rapidly moved up to over 40 per cent. Here at last, we might think, women have entered the 'economy'. No one can now claim that economics is about men. But assumptions about women's place die hard, and even as wage workers they appear peripheral. Two out of five are working part-time; three out of four are in service work; somehow they still get bypassed in economic debate. The economy conjures up a picture of high finance (men in the City) and industry (men in overalls). We think of full-time male workers, not part-time women workers; we think of jobs in manufacturing, not jobs in services. No one would be surprised if a meeting billed as 'The Crisis of the British Economy' focused exclusively on the decline in manufacturing. But there would certainly be complaints if the debate was all about the crisis in clerical work. Women and economics do not mix well together, and discussions about women all too often seem out of place in economic debate.

Today this has become an acute problem. In the present crisis socialists have turned increasingly to economics, and details of economic policy are more widely discussed than before. Socialists in the post-war Labour Party were perhaps less concerned with such issues. They built their dreams around the welfare state – an end to class privilege in education, a free health service based on need instead of money, a living minimum for all. The economy, it seemed, could be left to take care of itself, with just a little assistance from the state.

Outside the Labour Party some socialists condemned this emphasis on social issues, arguing that it evaded the basic question of who controls the economy. But they too avoided details. They put their faith in the abolition of private property and waxed impatient of more short-term reforms. Socialists divided into 'reformists' or 'revolutionaries', and neither side concerned itself with detailed programmes for economic change.

Over the past ten years discussion has shifted. Fewer now see the problem as a question of reform versus revolution and many have turned to the formulation of short-term policy. Socialist discussion has become an odd mixture of the visionary and the pragmatic. People concern themselves with a wide range of issues – the problems of sexism and racism, the dangers of nuclear war, the horrors of drudgery in work, the destruction of the environment. Side by side with this, attention has focused down on to the intricacies of policy, with matters of the economy increasingly to the fore.

Inside the Labour Party, for example, the 'alternative economic strategy' has appeared on the scene, setting new terms of reference. What kinds of policies will create full employment? How can we control a capitalist economy? How can we force banks and big business to fit in with national plans? Are we for or against import controls? Should we nationalise 20 or 200 companies? How can we make planning agreements stick? What can we do about the multinationals? Can we make use of pension funds to create more jobs in Britain? Over the years the list of questions has grown, but they are all economic ones and none of them asks about women.

However much socialists claim to have widened their horizons, once the subject of economics comes up the vision narrows again. Any woman who has sat in on a meeting about the economy will know the problem. Everything that seemed so crucial outside now appears irrelevant. 'What have women to do with economics?' The impatience is barely disguised.

Women's issues may well be important – but in their own place and time and *please*, not here.

Feminists have found this barrier hard to break, partly because we want to attack it from both sides. We want to challenge those ageing stereotypes that depict men as workers and women as housewives. We want to make people realise that times have changed, that women are now nearly half the labour force, that no economic strategy can work unless it takes note of this. We want to say that economics is about women, too; that they cannot be treated under social policy alone.

At the same time we want to question the narrowness of economics, redefine it so that it spans our lives outside work as well. Women work both inside and outside the home and we need an economics that can deal with that. People's needs do not fit into a neat home and work package, with social policies for the one and economic policies for the other. Our lives are too complex and interwoven. For women, one of the key problems is the *relationship* between waged work and child care – how can we organise work so that it fits with the demands of children? Operating with economic policy, on the one side, and social policy, on the other, we cannot properly cope with such questions. We need a new kind of economics.

Think of how jobs are organised today. Employers ignore their workers as people, pretending that each has a housewife in the background. When they take on a man for a job they do not want his personal history. Does he have three children or none? Who cares? The woman is supposed to deal with this problem: the demands of the children will be met by her.

The school day may end at 3.30 p.m. or 4 p.m., but how many men expect to leave work in time to pick up their children? The shops may close at 5.30 p.m. or 6 p.m, but which employers give their male workers time off to do the shopping? The electrician will call 'sometime in the morning'. The child has a toothache and has to go to the dentist. Jobs are not organised to meet such emergencies, and very few men get time off to cope with them. Few enough even get paternity leave when their children are born.

The whole set-up assumes a woman as housewife, yet everyone knows most women work. So what happens? Women somehow fit things in – thus taking jobs that can be combined with such responsibilities, they run around at break-neck speed to meet all demands. As long as we could imagine that most women were full-time housewives we could forget this problem. Today we can only forget it if we stick our heads in the sand.

Any strategy for the future has to challenge the dominance of jobs as currently defined. We can no longer continue with the idea that women will pick up the pieces. Just visualise for a moment a world where there were children but no women, and think what this would mean for the nature of work. Men's working hours would have to be cut, their shift-times would have to be altered, the rigidity of their work would have to go. If we are serious about equality for women, these are the kinds of changes we need to think about.

We have to adapt work to fit with the rest of our life, and particularly adapt it to fit with children. For the present, the adaptation is done by women; the price of having children is paid by the mothers. Why not a new approach? If the needs of children do not fit with the demands of full-time work, then the jobs must be changed.

For socialists involved in working out an economic strategy, such ideas seem dangerously demobilising. Many feel ill at ease when children enter the debate, and wish they could fall back as usual on the idea that this is women's concern. They fear that the hard cutting-edge of socialist alternatives could be blunted by female sentiment, and while prepared to support demands for more nurseries, prefer to keep this separate from economic affairs. They doubt the relevance of a new approach to work, when for millions today the key problem is no work at all.

They would rather focus on mechanisms for 'getting the economy right', seeing this as the first step to more radical alternatives. With a revived economy and more resources to spare, they argue, we could afford the luxury of these wider debates. But to get into the problem of changing capitalist

work *now*, when capitalism is deep in crisis, would be prema-
ture. First things first: first the nitty-gritty of the economy, then
the problem of women.

When feminists reject this argument, they are not saying
there is no problem of resources. It would make little sense to
push for an ambitious programme of social change without asking how we can pay for it. But we cannot assume the economy
is neutral between men and women. The way we choose to 'get
the economy right' can affect relations between the sexes. It
can confirm women in their inequality and dependence – or it
can begin to challenge these. If we treat the question as a
matter of stages (first the economy, then . . .) we imply that
equality is just the icing on the cake.

As many have argued, the labour movement's alternative
economic strategy tends in just this direction. It is a strategy for
restoring Britain to the economic growth and relatively full
employment that characterised the best of the post-war years.
It is relatively uncritical about the inequalities that also marked
those years.

As a programme for economic expansion it has relegated
women's issues to a separate sphere. Under the guise of a supposedly neutral strategy for all working people, it has presented a vision which fits most with the needs of working men.
Here, 'economics' has acted very much to marginalise women
– their concerns are treated as an additional package of social
policies, and the implications in terms of the nature of work
have been evaded. The strategy is mainly about restoring us to
pre-crisis conditions, and very little beyond that.

The following six chapters outline existing policies within the
labour movement, and feminist alternatives. Chapter 1 looks
at the characteristics of women's work today, both inside and
outside the home. It indicates some of the massive changes
now under way, as the full-time housewife recedes into history
and women workers edge up towards half of the labour force.
One implication, it argues, is that we must have strategies that
can deal with the relationship between waged work and the
rest of our lives.

Chapter 2 discusses the main alternative debated today – the labour movement's alternative economic strategy. It summarises some of the criticisms levelled by feminists, and shows the hidden male bias in much of the strategy.

Chapter 3 sets out some obvious points for action if we are to talk seriously about women's right to work. Furthermore, it argues that the right to work is not enough, and that the real question is the kind of work there is.

Chapter 4 is really the key chapter and develops the demand for a shorter working week, as one route to equality between men and women.

Chapter 5 looks at the continuing assumption that men are the breadwinners and women the dependants, and argues that this is a major stumbling-block to sexual equality. It outlines various changes in tax and social security that could begin to shift this pattern of dependence.

Chapter 6 criticises free collective bargaining as it is currently practised and argues for an end to low pay and an attack on differentials. It assesses the relative importance of union action versus state regulation, and argues for a legal minimum wage.

1.

Between Two Worlds

Women's oppression is a familiar story and much of it starts with the sharp divide between what men and women do. 'Different but equal' has never been a convincing slogan. When women are praised for their feminine qualities, there is usually a smirk behind the praise. When they are advised to stick to their womanly sphere, there is often contempt behind the advice. When we hear something described as 'women's work' we can be sure this means good enough for women and not good enough for men.

Getting status from the job you do is not peculiar to capitalism, and neither is the pattern that puts women's work lower than men's. In all societies there has been a hierarchy, with some jobs counting for more than others. Often enough this has coincided with a sexual division of labour – the tasks women do carrying less status than those done by men.

In 'hunting and gathering' societies, for example, hunting (male) has a higher status than gathering (female). Gender divisions are usually quite rigid, and though in many societies young men share the work of women, adult men move on to better things. So building and repairing a house might be men's work; agriculture often women's. Where men and women work together in agriculture there is normally a clear demarcation of tasks: men perhaps responsible for tending the crops that are sold on the market, while women get on with growing the food crops; or the men ploughing the fields while women look after the poultry. Exactly which jobs fall on men and which on women has varied enormously, but the pattern of segregation runs through all known societies. And where there *is* a division of labour between the sexes, men's work usually counts for more.

For most people the main novelty in capitalism is that work is more sharply divided from the rest of life. In previous societies the hours worked were dictated by the nature of the task rather than the demands of the employer. Instead of a fixed working day, people had a fixed set of things to do. As capitalism established its dominance it brought in a stricter separation between work and leisure, so that, with the crucial exception of housewives, most workers now know exactly how long they must work. They go out to work, home to play; they work in these hours and not in those.

When you are employed by someone else your hours of work are fixed before you start, your wages agreed and your tasks decided for you. Time-keeping begins to matter for the first time and the clock begins to dominate our lives. In slave societies slaves could be called on to work at any time. In feudal societies serfs had to till the land according to the demands of the seasons. In capitalism you turn up to work at the agreed time and clock off at the end of the day.

This may look like a great liberation. Instead of a working day that could be anything from two to 20 hours, we now have a definite working day, and once we have finished we are free to spend our time as we will.

But the work has been invasive. It is the employers who decide what hours we work, and for those on shift systems, hours are set to satisfy the demands of the machines. Inside those hours sold to their bosses, workers face a never-ending barrage of new techniques, as employers cast around for ways of raising the productivity of work. Once they saw the limits in lengthening the working day, employers turned their attention to getting more out of those hours left at their disposal. Capitalism thrives on more for less, and once pinned to a working week of 40 or 50 hours, with wages higher than basic subsistence, has had to do its best with what it has. The pace of work has increased steadily over the past century, so that for many 'leisure' time is simply time for recuperation. People barely have time to recover from one day's pressure before going on to the next.

Domestic labour

With such a dense working day, what happens to the incessant demands of child care and housework? All that cooking, cleaning, mending, shopping, washing that has to go on for each household? These of course are done by women, who in their role as housewives have somehow escaped both the trials and benefits of capitalist work. Unlike other workers, women in the home have no boss standing over them telling them what to do. The husband and children may well complain if the housewife slackens her efforts, but the real compulsion to work often comes from the housewives themselves. As is frequently said, housewives seem to exploit themselves by their own high standards – and these standards often cut across the criteria of capitalist efficiency.

Capitalism usually tries to cut the amount of time workers spend on any one task, to get more output from each hour's work. Women working in the home often seem to aim at the opposite. The lavishly prepared meal is preferred over the one thrown together from convenience foods; the carefully polished surfaces are more highly valued than washable plastic. Women are kept at their daily grind by mechanisms more complex than the supervisor in a factory. They are compelled by their own need to prove their worth, by long years of socialisation at the hands of their mothers, by the fear of male complaints. They will not be sacked if their output falls below the norm – and to this extent they have it easier than those who go out to work. But if they drop their standards too much, they might lose respect, the love of their man, or, at worst, his financial support. The controls are vague but powerful.

Unlike most other work under capitalism, domestic labour still has no clear demarcations between work and leisure. Looking after a child is a 24-hour business; it means being on the job – though not actually working – all that time. There is no beginning and no end to the working day. With young children in the house, even going to bed is not the end of it.

When surveys estimate how long housewives work, the totals are astonishing. Women working in the home do hours that most wage workers would reject out of hand. Those with young children are said to average 77 hours each week, just on those recurrent chores of shopping, cooking, cleaning, mending, washing, and so on and on . . .

Partly because there is no clear divide between work and leisure, the hours mount up. There sometimes seems no limit to the time spent in housework. During the post-war boom women were inundated with labour-saving devices: vacuum cleaners, washing machines, food mixers, a host of commodities for cutting domestic labour. These innovations have made little difference to total labour time. Women now spend more of their time shopping and looking after children, less of their time cleaning and dusting. But full-time housewives today work as long as their mothers and grandmothers used to do.

Again, this is connected to the fact that housework is not like other jobs. When a typist reads a novel on the job she feels no shame; when a housewife finds herself with time on her hands she often feels guilty. Labour-saving devices have not, on the whole, saved time. They have simply upped the standards. Take washing clothes. Over the past 50 years the technology has been revolutionised: most households have running hot and cold water; many have washing machines; some have clothes dryers; many of the clothes we wear are made of fabrics that need no ironing. Yet women spend more time washing clothes today than they used to do. Washing machines have meant more frequent washes; food mixers more exacting recipes; vacuum cleaners higher standards of cleanliness.

Of course, if housewives were *paid* for their work there would be no end of productivity schemes to make them more efficient. But because the work has never been waged their time has no cost. Housewives have to be maintained whether they do 10 hours a week or 100, so how long they work seems a matter of no concern.

Unequal partners

Sometimes housewives seem an archaic throwback to days before capitalism – workers who have no fixed hours, no supervisor overseeing their work, and also no wages. In fact full-time housewives are an invention of capitalism, but the kind of work they do seems out of place. As some feminists have said, women working in the home look more like slaves in ancient society than wage workers in modern capitalism. They work for a particular individual (the husband) and depend on his goodwill for their keep.

If they worked for anyone else – cooking for the man down the road whose wife has left him, perhaps – they would expect payment. Or if the state organised house-cleaning services like it organises road-cleaning, it would have to pay its workers. But when a woman does these tasks in the privacy of her own home she gets no wage. What she gets is an income, a part share of her husband's wage.

As breadwinner of the family the man is supposed to earn a family wage, high enough to support not just himself but a full-time wife and children. Only a tiny proportion of households now fit this model, but it is still widely regarded as a norm. The man will hand over part of his (family) wage to his wife, but the wage rewards *his* labour not hers. As surveys of household accounts regularly show, the money is not shared equally. Because he is the breadwinner the man can stake his claim to extras – money for 'his' car, for drinking with his friends, for luxuries over and above basic living. The way the wage packet is divided varies considerably from one household to another, but many women have complained that higher wages are not passed on in higher housekeeping money.

The partnership between husband and wife masks a deep inequality. Women work longer hours than men and get less for it. Their main work is unwaged and so not considered real work. 'What do you do?' 'I'm just a housewife.' The endless chores implied in this phrase will not qualify the women as real workers.

Domestic labour is necessary to society (food has to be prepared, houses have to maintained, children have to be cared for) but is rarely valued. Even child care gets a low status, though it may enjoy that weird mixture of contempt – anyone can do it – and reverence – being a mother is the greatest experience there is – that marks contemporary attitudes to women. Women's work is not real work and women can expect no reward in the shape of a wage.

Women and waged work

The fact that work is such a different experience for men and for women carries over into the jobs women do outside the home. The vast majority of women go out to work at some time in their lives. Single women are as likely to have jobs as single men; half of all married women go out to work; one-quarter of women with children under five go out to work.

These women live on the margins of two worlds, where the demands of children, husband and home constantly compete with the demands of the job. Men live more firmly in one; though they, too, may spend many hours working in the home – maintaining the house or garden – this work will never interfere with their real (paid) jobs. It has to fit in around waged work, whereas for women waged work has to fit itself around family responsibilities. The result is that many women work part-time while many men work overtime. And even when women do work full-time (over 30 hours) the hours they work are lower than men's. The 1982 *New Earnings Survey* showed 31 per cent of full-time women working less than 36 hours each week, but only 11.6 per cent of men. At the other end of the scale, 35.8 per cent of men worked more than 40 hours each week, compared with only 7.4 per cent of women.

Women's working hours have been formally restricted by law, but a much more fundamental constraint is their role as mothers. The hundreds of thousands of women working as homeworkers, the two out of every five working part-time, the office cleaners working through the night so they can take care of their children by day, the factory workers starting at 7 a.m. so they can pick up the children from school in the afternoon

– all these are fitting their jobs around their children and household tasks.

Some quarter of a million women take in work to do in the home. Trapped by the needs of small children or sick relatives, these women work long hours for pitiful wages – sewing garments, assembling toys, addressing envelopes, making knitwear. They have none of the legal rights won by trade unionists in normal jobs. They can be sacked at will, have no claim to holiday pay, maternity leave or pensions, and, of course, no right to complain about the safety of their working conditions. Some have won rights under the Employment Protection Act, getting at least compensation for unfair dismissal. But the vast majority work under Dickensian conditions, producing goods which are often sold at high prices in 'quality' shops.

As well as this hidden army of homeworkers (no official figures tell us exactly how many there are) are the large numbers of women working part-time. Two out of five women with jobs are working 30 hours or less a week, with varying degrees of job insecurity. Like the homeworkers, they are constrained into this kind of work by the demands of child care: about two-thirds of the women working part-time have dependent children.

They are slightly better protected than homeworkers. If they work 16 hours or more a week they have the same legal rights as any full-time worker, and if they work less than 16 they may still qualify after 5 years with the same employer. But they are usually excluded from employers' pension schemes and can count themselves lucky if they get any holiday pay. Nearly 20 per cent of Britain's labour force is now part-time (by far the highest proportion in Europe), and some of these workers have been doing the same job for 15 years or more. But part-timers are still overwhelmingly regarded as casual workers.

When it comes to wages, part-time workers get a raw deal. Their rates of pay are rarely proportional to full-time wages, and the supposedly encouraging rise in women's pay relative to men's would give less cause for optimism if the earnings of part-time workers were taken into account. Hour by hour, full-time women workers get only three-quarters the pay of full-time men workers; *part*-timers (nearly all women) get less than 60 per cent of the hourly rate of full-time men. But forced as they are to take jobs that can fit with the needs of children and housework, women often have no choice but to take these wages.

Women's wages

Women carry the consequences of housework and children into most of the jobs they do. As well as constraining their choice of job, their 'role' seems to drag down wages even for full-time women workers. For as far back as we know, women were stuck with wages of around 60 per cent of average male rates, and only with the Equal Pay Act did this begin to change. The Act was passed in 1970, in force by 1975, and by 1977 women's pay had moved up to 76.6 per cent of men's. The figure only compares hourly rates for full-time workers over the age of 21, and so considerably exaggerates the gains. Even for these workers the rate fell back again to 74.7 per cent in 1980 and rose marginally to 75.1 per cent in 1982.

Because men and women do such different jobs, the Equal Pay Act has a limited scope. It works best where men and women work side by side in the same job – here discrimination is obvious and employers are more easily forced to pay equal rates. But in Britain today – as in so many societies throughout so much of history – women do women's work and men do men's. Many jobs are almost exclusively female – nursing, for example, typing, canteen work, machining – and in these there are no higher-paid men to push up overall wages. Half of men are in jobs where the workforce is 90 per cent male; half of women in jobs where the workforce is 70 per cent female. Existing legislation offers little to these, and in some cases made matters worse. Many employers seized their chances to move men out of jobs where they worked alongside women, and since it took five years to phase the Act in, there was plenty of time to do this. The result is that many workplaces are *more* segregated on sexual lines now than they were before the Equal Pay Act.

Equal Pay has not meant equal pay, and while people continue to debate the exact causes of low pay for women, two points seem clear. First, the jobs women do are consistently undervalued just because women do them. Women are only housewives, doing work anyone could do, so the jobs they take on outside the home cannot be worth much. This certainly colours the way service jobs are treated in our society. Most women work in the service sector and the jobs they do there – cleaning, cooking, nursing, social work – are often treated as natural extensions of their caring role in the home. These jobs are supposed to come easy to women, hence they get little status and low pay.

The worst-paid women's jobs are the ones that involve servicing others, the ones that look most like all those tasks women do in the home for free. So hairdressers, kitchen hands, waitresses, cleaners, home helps, all these find themselves at the bottom of the scale. Once overtime payments are taken into account, they earn considerably less than the lowest-paid men workers (see Table 1).

Table 1   **Average gross weekly earnings for lowest-paid female occupations** (full-time workers in 1982)

	Excluding overtime	Including overtime	Those with total earnings below £100 (%)
Hairdressers	55.90	56.00	98.7
Barmaids	61.60	65.90	93.8
Kitchen hands	62.90	67.90	91.1
Waitresses	63.00	66.40	92.4
Shop assistants	65.60	66.60	96.2
Counter hands	66.60	72.30	90.0
Check-out operators	67.40	69.60	94.4
Cleaners	67.50	73.70	89.7
Home, domestic helpers	69.20	75.40	89.4
Sewing machinists (textiles)	70.50	71.50	91.4

Source: *New Earnings Survey*, 1982.

The lowest-paid male jobs also reflect this undervaluing of domestic type work, though here the pattern is less strict. Also, because most men do overtime, few find themselves with such pitifully low wages (see Table 2).

Table 2 **Average gross weekly earnings for lowest-paid male occupations** (full-time workers in 1982)

	Excluding overtime	Including overtime	Those with total earnings below £100 (%)
Bar workers	81.90	94.60	62.3
General farm workers	82.90	95.10	65.5
Agricultural machinery drivers	84.90	102.70	53.1
Hospital porters	87.10	102.20	51.5
Road sweepers	87.80	97.20	68.7
Caretakers	88.20	101.60	58.9
Stock workers (agriculture)	90.40	111.10	41.9
Butchers, meat cutters	91.20	98.00	62.1
Cleaners	92.00	104.30	53.7
Gardeners/groundsmen	93.90	100.70	55.4

Source: *New Earnings Survey*, 1982.

The pay we get is supposed to reflect how skilled the work is, but more often it reflects the sex of the workers. Even those jobs which involve a long training may not be regarded as really skilled when they are done by women. Nurses, for example, get a lot of public sympathy for their long hours and dedication. But as any man who chooses to train as a nurse will know, the job itself does not have a high status. The work is women's work, and, by virtue of that, downgraded.

The same pattern appears even in jobs that have no obvious parallel with domestic labour. It may take months to train a good typist, but because typing is so typically a 'women's job' it ends up low down on the scale. It is not just that women do unskilled jobs – their jobs *become* unskilled because women do them.

The second point about women's low pay is much more peculiar to capitalism. People justify poor wages for women on the grounds that women are not the real breadwinners. Men, it is said, are entitled to higher pay because they have a wife and children to support. They need a 'family wage'. Women, it is argued, are not the main breadwinners, and their earnings are only a supplement to household income. Why should they get wages as high as those paid to men?

In principle, these arguments should be heard no longer: the Equal Pay Act says that men and women should get the same wage for the same work. But while women are segregated into women's jobs and men into men's, it has been possible to keep on paying women lower wages. Now the low pay is justified because of the nature of the job, not because the workers are women. The principle may have changed, but the reality is depressingly familiar.

Taking it all together it begins to look like a package deal. As mothers and housewives women work long hours for little reward. They get no real status in a world which equates value with wages, and no hope of clocking off at the end of the day. Because of domestic responsibilities they are limited in the jobs they can do, and considered unworthy of high wages. Because their working lives are constantly interrupted by pregnancy and child care they lose out on training and promotion. Consequently, in those jobs with a career structure women remain concentrated on the lower rungs of the ladder. Women account for 80 per cent of primary school teachers – but only 50 per cent of primary school head teachers. Even when women squeeze their way into the more skilled and better-paid jobs, they rarely rise to the top.

The changing shape of the economy

All these features of women's work are well known. House-work and child care, homework and part-time work, unskilled, low-paid jobs – the list is a familiar one and often recited. But within this familar pattern a new shape is emerging. The British economy is not just declining, but changing fast – and one crucial change has been the increase in women's wage employment.

Since the 1950s women have been going out to work on an unprecedented scale. As already mentioned, from making up around 30 per cent of the labour force, they have moved up to over 40 per cent, with a startling rise in the numbers of married women who work. Though most women still give up their jobs when their children are young, they now return after a few years. Single mothers (now about one million of the population) often cannot afford even a temporary break from employment. The full-time housewife is increasingly rare. Most women are wage-earners, combining housework, child care and jobs in what is known as the 'double shift'. There have been major changes in the working pattern of women, most of them as yet unnoticed in socialist debate.

Women dominate the service sector that has grown up since the second world war. As health and education expanded, it was women who came forward to work as teachers and nurses. As leisure activities boomed, it was women who staffed the restaurants, pubs and hotels. As the size of both public and private corporations increased, it was women who took on the myriad clerical tasks.

The shape of the workforce has thus been dramatically redrawn. Twenty years ago manual workers made up nearly 66 per cent of the working population; now the figure is just over 50 per cent. Twenty years ago 36 per cent of all jobs were in manufacturing; now this is down to 28 per cent. The number of craft workers has declined; the number of professional workers – in health, say, or education – has gone up. Through all these changes the place of women in the wage economy has expanded.

The older industries that were so much the basis of the British economy – mining, ship-building, steel – were almost exlusively male. These have been decimated in recent years, and much of the new industrial growth has been in sectors that employ women. Electronics assembly and instrument engineering have drawn extensively on female labour, so that even though most women still work in services, a sizeable proportion now work in the new manufacturing industries.

Where people work has also changed. For manufacturing and clerical work alike the trend is towards decentralisation. Firms have moved out of the big cities, where rents are high and workers well organised. They have opened factories and offices in smaller towns. New technology makes for easier communication, and employers can now offload the more routinised work to the regions, while keeping their head offices and research departments in London or the South East.

New industries have avoided traditional centres of labour strength and sought out 'green labour' in the rural areas. East Anglia has enjoyed relative growth; the West Midlands has joined the older declining regions as an area of high unemployment. Older industries have moved too, exploring new territories in their search for cheaper labour. In all these developments, more women have been employed.

Take the clothing industry, discussed by Doreen Massey in her article 'The shape of things to come':

> In the 1960s it was caught in a vice. It was under competition from low-cost imports. But its own usual supply of women workers in the urban areas (particularly London) was threatened by expansion of the service sector. Big firms in the industry solved the dilemma by changing location. New sources of labour, more vulnerable and with fewer alternative sources of employment, were sought out. The new source of labour was older, married women, the new locations were smaller towns, trading estates and sometimes quite isolated locations in the peripheral regions of the country – the rural areas such as the South West and old heavy-industry areas such as the coalfields.

So in the mining areas men were losing their jobs and women were being taken on, often for the first time, in manufacturing industry.

It is in these areas of traditional male employment that the most breath-taking changes have occured. In Wales there has been a dramatic transformation. Until the early 1960s, less than one in three Welsh women went out to work, considerably lower than the proportion working in the rest of Britain. By 1981 this was closer to two in three. The massive destruction of 'male' jobs in mining, the unparelleled expansion of 'female' work in services, the arrival of multinationals greedy for women workers, all these have conspired to reshape the Welsh working class. On present trends, women workers will out-number men in less than 10 years.

Living on the margins

Even on the traditional definition of the economy, which blandly ignores the work in the home, women are now right in there at the heart of the British economy. But few have admitted the significance of this. Women, it seems, are defined as housewives whatever they do, and mere facts have not been enough to change this. If they go out to work this is still treated as peripheral to their main role in life. And because many work part-time and most in the service sector, their jobs are still not regarded as real.

There are two lessons to be drawn from this. One is the almost incredible blindness of the labour movement – and more broadly the socialist movement – to the existence of women. It is not so long ago that we used to hear the phrase 'workers and their wives' – as though no woman ever went out to work. Even today people talk of the working class as if it were exclusively male, made up of miners not nurses, car-workers not typists. The imagery of trade union struggle is still one of muscular, toil-burdened men. We talk of blue-collar and white-collar workers, a distinction derived entirely from male dress. The worker is male. Indeed, this assumption is so powerful that I have to refresh myself constantly with the statistics of women's work. A moment's absentmindedness and I fall back again into the illusion that women are only house-wives and mothers.

The second lesson is that no strategy can work today if it focuses exclusively on either home or work. Women span both worlds, and in doing so they demand a strategy that embraces both. It is no good dealing with just one or the other.

The recent experience of women has called the whole nature of waged work into question. While waged work was male and domestic work female (never a neat divide, but at one time more convincing than it is today) we could happily forget their relationship. Men had their world of work, unions and pubs; women their world of house, babies and gossip. Now that so many struggle to survive on the margins of these two worlds, the mismatch becomes a burning issue.

2.

An Alternative Economic Strategy?

The feminist Rebecca West once said, 'when a socialist takes to being dull, he is much duller than anyone else'. For many, the alternative economic strategy (AES) is further evidence of this. It calls for a radical extension of planning, and to that extent is a novelty in British politics. But in terms of its goals and overall vision, it contains nothing dramatically new. Its opponents dismiss it as an old-fashioned Keynesianism, a dogged refusal to face facts. Critics in the women's movement have been equally damning: they have argued it sets its goals by the needs of male workers, offering little to women.

The alternative economic strategy is marked by its predecessor, the post-war boom, and I would sum it up crudely as an attempt to recapture the gains of that period. In those fantasy years, capitalism tried to convince us it had finished with crisis. Britain, along with the rest of the advanced capitalist world, reached high rates of growth in the 1950s and 1960s – and this time, benefits were passed on to workers. The consumer goods industries became the dynamic centre of the economy. Cars, washing machines, television sets, refrigerators, consumer durables in their millions were all produced at prices low enough for workers to buy them. Mass unemployment was wiped out, more and more people were drawn into the labour market, many married women found jobs for the first time. As output rose, so too did wages, and the higher wages in their turn encouraged more production. A rising spiral of self-sustaining growth emerged, with expansion here feeding further growth there, and so on in an endless pattern. It looked as if it could last for ever.

The rewards were not, as we know, shared equally. The economy was greedy for more labour, but it paid its new workers – women and immigrants – less than its old. They usually found themselves at the bottom of the ladder with little hope of climbing up. The gap between low-paid and high-paid remained much as before, and many still lived in poverty. But somehow these problems stayed below the surface: with so much to go around we could imagine that everyone was sharing the gains.

Crisis

The boom did not go on for ever and, by the late 1960s the rate of growth world-wide started to slow down. The twin problems of unemployment and inflation began to appear. The numbers out of work in Britain reached one million in 1972, and inflation averaged 8 to 9 per cent a year through the 1970s. Post-war growth was dependent on certain conditions, and it became clear that capitalism could not guarantee their permanence.

Most importantly, the boom relied on a steady growth in productivity – only with this could profits and wages keep rising in harmony. At the beginning, this seemed possible. Assembly-line techniques offered massive productivity gains in the new consumer goods industries, most typically in the production of cars. But by the mid-1960s these were reaching their limit.

Assembly lines operate by closing the gaps in the working day, keeping the workers in continuous motion and cutting 'time-wasting' to the minimum. Teams of time-and-motion experts were sent out to scrutinise the workers and draw up plans for eliminating their 'unnecessary' movements. Bottlenecks between one part of the factory and another were unblocked. The line was speeded up. Time off for tea breaks or going to the toilet was carefully monitored. Anything that could extract more output from each working day was tried.

Eventually, a limit was reached. Beyond a certain intensity workers just stop working, and if things get worse they simply stay away. By the 1970s the car industry had become famous for its high rate of absenteeism, its frequent unofficial stoppages, its rapid labour turnover. Employers began to talk about 'job enrichment' – a sure sign they were facing a problem – and some firms, like the Volvo plant in Sweden, went so far as to abandon the assembly line. Productivity gains became more and more difficult, and though output per worker continued to rise, it was not at the rate of earlier years. As a share of output, profits in manufacturing fell in the 1960s and continued to fall even more dramatically through the 1970s.

Outside these most dynamic sectors, further problems were brewing. As right-wing politicians keep reminding us, the post-war years saw a massive rise in public spending, much of it on social services. As a proportion of Britain's annual output, public spending went up from less than 26 per cent in 1937 to 45 per cent in 1951, and 58 per cent in 1975. Social services – mainly health, education, housing and social security benefits – accounted for almost half of this. The increase partly reflected improved services: more people became eligible for social security payments; health and education were freely available to all; the state laid on new services, like home helps or meals on wheels, to compensate for the married women who now went out to work. But much of the increase was simply to do with the changing age structure of the population. The number of young and old people who had to be supported by the working population went up, from 49 dependants for each 100 working people in 1941 to 66 by 1969.

No one really knows how the productivity improvements in these sectors compare with those in private industry. The National Accounts simply measure the output of public services by the numbers of people they employ, thereby assuming that the productivity of these workers never changes. Administrators in the public services have their own measures of productivity, but these tell us little about either the quality or the efficiency of the service. As David Hall points out in *The Cuts Machine*, administrators in the NHS assess efficiency by the level of bed occupancy – how much of the time a hospital bed is filled by a patient.

> A simple way of improving this ratio is just to cut the number of beds, so that there are always patients desperately needing to fill them. This might be a great way to get the most out of a bed, but it is not what most people regard as an improvement in health services.

We are encouraged to think of these services as a drain on the economy, but have no sure way of saying whether they save us money or not. Nevertheless, it seems likely that productivity in public services cannot match developments in the mass consumer industries, if only because we want different things from them. The work is not standardised like the production of washing machines, and usually we like it that way. We want personal service rather than number counting. We want more teachers for each school, not fewer; more doctors in each hospital, not fewer. As our demands over the quality of services increase, so too does the cost.

Taking these together we can see the scale of the problem. Full employment, rising real wages, better social services were all premised on capital getting enough to keep it happy. But with productivity touching its limits in the leading sectors and the relative costs of services beginning to soar, the post-war boom began to seem like a fantasy. Self-sustaining growth was only on the agenda for a couple of decades, and by the end of that we were heading for the most serious world crisis since the 1930s. In the 1950s we were led to believe it could last for ever. Now we are told to reduce our expectations, tighten our belts, and adjust ourselves to what we can afford.

The labour movement's alternative

The alternative economic strategy (AES) was an early response to this. Its first outlines were worked out in the 1970s and many of its key elements found their way into the Labour Party Programme in 1973. The basic idea was that private capital had become too powerful and that the time was ripe for a major shift to public control. Too few firms controlled too much output. The top 100 accounted for nearly half Britain's manufacturing production, and all the signs were that this share would increase. Faced with such massive, often multinational companies, the state had little leverage over the economy. Existing techniques were too indirect, too feeble. The government could put the interest rate up or down, raise or lower company taxes, offer incentives to attract firms to poorer regions. But it could not tell the companies what to do. In the new era of monopoly power, only direct action would work.

So the AES called for planned investment and growth, on a scale unknown in peace-time Britain. One novelty of the strategy was that it threw up new ways of asserting public control: the old demand for nationalisation was still there, but mixed in with other ideas. Certain industries should be fully nationalised: ship-building, aircraft production, perhaps even pharmaceuticals. Leading firms in other sectors should be bought out and put under the umbrella of a state holding company (the National Enterprise Board). Those big firms still left in private hands should be controlled through planning agreements, drawn up in discussion with government and unions.

With a new framework of planning mechanisms, it was argued, the government could tackle the root cause of the crisis, which, according to most supporters of the AES, was falling investment. Private firms had failed to reinvest, or else chosen to move themselves overseas. Left to the mercies of unplanned capitalism, no wonder investment and productivity fell. But with planning once in force, we could lay the foundations of economic revival.

The state would take charge of technological innovations, providing an impetus through its own nationalised sectors, and pressurising private employers to fall in line. Massive injections of new investment would stimulate growth. British industry would be rescued from decades of neglect.

Industrial democracy would secure the support of trade unionists, who instead of resisting technological change would begin to promote it. Faced with employers who put their own interests first, of course workers block change. Just to protect themselves they insist rigidly on the demarcation between one job and another, refuse new technology, resist anything new. But once protected by a government that pursues their interests and promises them more say in decisions, they will participate readily in raising productivity.

Socialists have continued to refine the strategy and under the shadow of rising unemployment further issues have become urgent. Job creation is now a major priority and today's strategy calls for an immediate and dramatic rise in public spending, reversing recent cuts and creating many new jobs overnight.

Supporters of the strategy have turned their attention to the problem of inflation – how can we be sure the gains of more jobs will not be lost in higher prices? People have argued for price controls, perhaps even (a touchy subject here) wage controls. People have advocated import controls – or 'planned trade', as many prefer to say. Further debates have opened up: How to control the City? What to do with pension funds? The range of issues has broadened year by year, so that many now say there is no single strategy. There are many strategies, united by a belief in planning and a hope of short-term gains.

What about the women?

Where do women fit into this? As half the population they will of course share in the gains of economic growth. As those with the greatest interest in public services (both as workers and as consumers) they should be particularly enthusiastic about an expansion in public spending. Beyond this, the strategy makes no obvious gesture in their direction.

It contents itself with economics in the narrowest sense, talking only of jobs that are done for wages and mainly of products that are sold on the market. It has nothing to say about the work that goes on in the home, and nothing about the relationship between this and waged work. It does talk about better social services, but more with a view to boosting demand and stimulating growth than because these services can improve the quality of our lives. Finally, it is not a strategy for *equality* but for growth. It talks of how to get back to the 'good old days' and ignores how bad these were for many women and low-paid workers.

We could just leave the criticism at that. The alternative economic strategy is a strategy for growth; what we want is a strategy for equality. But supporters of the AES will easily dismiss such complaints. We know, they will say, that this programme is not everything. We do not pretend it adds up to a fully fledged socialism, and we never suggested it would solve the problems of women. Nevertheless, it is a start. So while we continue our debates about the best way to an equal society, why not join the campaign for an alternative that can at least save jobs?

The answer is that the strategy is both inadequate *and* biased. It is not a neutral strategy, but one that tends to identify the economy with men. On three important issues it leads us away from the needs and experience of women, moving us in a direction that could solidify existing inequalities.

Jobs for the boys

The first point is that it talks of full employment in a way that means full employment for men. For women, the problem is not just the number of jobs going – more fundamentally, it is a matter of the kind of jobs. Women are trapped in low-paid ghettos of monotonous, boring work: they need a strategy that deals in quality as well as quantity.

If men were offered the kind of full employment that capitalism gave women in the post-war boom, they would reject it out of hand. I would get short shrift if I stood up in a meeting and said everyone could have a job tomorrow if only they worked part-time or for three-quarters their normal pay. Yet this is what 'full employment' has meant for women. Two out of five work part-time; their wages lag far behind men's; even comparing the hourly rates for full-timers, they get only three-quarters of the average male pay. Add in the overtime rates for men and the bonuses they are more likely to get in the kind of jobs they do, and the gap is even greater. Add in the much lower hourly rates for part-timers, and the gap is greater still. Women often have to accept terms that would be scorned by men.

The question is not just one of the number of jobs. We should also be asking: What jobs? How well paid? No one wants full employment with massive wage cuts. No one wants full employment at any price. If this is so, then we have to question the price women currently pay for the chance of a job. How can we break down the extraordinary division between men's and women's work? How can we end the pattern that keeps women at the bottom of each ladder? How can we ensure girls get the same chance of apprenticeships as boys? How can we tackle women's low pay? Unless we take up these questions we have not even begun on a strategy of full employment for women. We are simply talking about jobs for the boys.

Industrial democracy

The second example of male bias comes in the discussion of industrial democracy. Industrial democracy, workers' participation, even occasionally workers' control – all these terms appear in today's debates and all of them sound good. The AES is full of fine intentions about planning from the bottom up instead of the top down. The TUC–Labour Party Liaison Committee has produced a document on *Economic and Industrial Democracy* which calls for 'the full involvement of working people' and a 'radical extension of industrial democracy'. Trade unionists in many industries have already staked a claim over workplace decisions. They demand a voice in deciding the pace of work, the movement of workers from one job to another, the operation of any disciplinary procedures. The planning document argues that such powers be extended to include a voice in company plans. Trade unionists should have the right to information on company finances and future plans, the right to consultation over closures, the right to representation at all levels within the company. As well as this, they should have a place on a national planning body which could co-ordinate all the different plans.

This sounds all very well, but does it really mean the full involvement of *all* working people? There is an unspoken bias here towards male workers. It is the full-time unionised workers in large companies who have the most to gain, and the majority of these are men. If industrial democracy becomes the only mechanism for popular involvement in planning, it will affect men and women unequally.

What about the women working at home, as housewives or homeworkers? What about the women working part-time with little chance of getting involved in their union? What about the women working in small shops and non-unionised workplaces? If planning *is* to be for all, we need more than workplace democracy. We need other opportunities for popular involvement.

The fact that these are more difficult to set up makes the discussion that much more urgent. Some local authorities have already taken steps in this direction. The Greater London Council now has a Popular Planning Unit, working on broader forms of popular involvement in planning decisions; many local councils have set up women's committees to allow women a voice in influencing local decisions. But these initiatives are fragile beside the long-established trade unions, and unless they are taken up more widely they will remain fringe concerns. Greater democracy will come to mean greater democracy for men.

Manufacturing versus services

The third problem in the AES is its emphasis on manufacturing. This is a tricky one and comes back to the notion of 'getting the economy right'. Many supporters of the strategy identify the decline in manufacturing as the key to the present crisis. This is where, they argue, Britain's ruling class has been at its most inept. It has taken the easy option of overseas investment and allowed a steady decline in British manufacturing. Right-wing parties may be wedded to the ideals of patriotism, but the capitalists they serve have other interests at heart. When higher profits are possible, capital simply leaves the country.

The statistics here are dramatic. Between 1970 and 1979 the number of jobs in manufacturing fell by 17 per cent, from 8,164,000 to 6,805,000. In London alone, a staggering 400,000 manufacturing jobs were lost between 1971 and 1981 – a decline of 37 per cent. The very fact that women have moved up to nearly half the labour force is part and parcel of this. The post-war years saw falling employment in (male) manufacturing and rising employment in (female) services.

The policies of the Tory government have been devastating for this sector. It has dropped what little controls there were on the movement of capital overseas, making it even easier for money to escape. High interest rates have discouraged firms from taking out loans for new investment, and forced many of them to the wall. A high exchange rate for the pound initially made Britain's exports more expensive than those of other countries, hitting manufacturing exports particularly hard. In the first four years of Thatcherite policies manufacturing output fell by almost 20 per cent.

With figures like these it is no wonder that the AES sets great store by the revival of manufacturing. But the effect is to push women out of the picture. Women work in services, men in manufacturing. Apart from electrical engineering, electronics, clothing, and the food, drink and tobacco industries, relatively few women work in manufacturing. Three out of four are in services like catering, hairdressing, cleaning, health, education, the retail trade. By focusing on manufacturing, the AES makes these seem like an extra paid for out of 'real' production.

It suggests that wealth is created in manufacturing, spent in services, that the jobs men do pay for those done by women. Given the coincidence of men/manufacturing, women/services, it is easy to suspect some male bias here. Is this yet another example of the 'men in overalls' syndrome? Is it that unquestioning assumption that the problems of the economy equals problems of men? Is there even a hint of a suggestion that the rise in women's employment has been at the expense of men's, that the time has come to redress the balance?

The idea that some sectors create wealth while others spend

it is deeply embedded in our ideology, but has little substantial basis. If the idea is that only private industry creates wealth, this seems a non-starter. That would mean that the nationalisation of coal turned mining into a non-productive sector – something that few would want to argue. If the idea is that only those goods and services sold on the market count as wealth, this again seems pretty shaky. That would mean that private medicine was productive, while the NHS is unproductive. Public services are a crucial part of the nation's wealth: without education there would be no skilled workers to run the offices and factories; without health there might be no workers at all.

Once we discount the 'real work and real things' argument – as though nursing is less real than making a table – there are only two good reasons for an emphasis on manufacturing. First, it matters because of the pattern of Britain's trade, which currently relies heavily on the export of manufactured goods. As long as Britain wants to buy things from the rest of the world (and few relish the notion of a Britain cut off from world trade) we need manufacturing exports to pay for them. This could of course change. Right now, oil exports are more prominent than they used to be, and in the future exports of services could become more important. But for the present this is one reason for a concern with manufacturing.

The second reason is that growth in manufacturing seems to stimulate the economy into faster growth overall. It seems to act as an 'engine for growth'. In both West and East Europe, when manufacturing output goes up, the total output of the economy goes up twice as fast. But this, too, is not immutable. Some of it stems from the point already made – that we have no reliable measure of output in the public services. In Britain we simply measure output in this sector by the numbers of people employed. It may be that output grows less quickly than in manufacturing – given the nature of the work, this seems quite plausible. But we have no way of knowing for sure.

The important thing is not to glorify manufacturing as if this is the only sector that produces wealth. Common sense today is full of notions of real and unreal work, and we should not give added weight to these. Cuts in public spending have been justified by the argument that social services are simply a drain on our resources. We have been told that wealth is created in the private sector, spent in the public; or created in manufacturing, spent in services. Socialists have their own prejudices here, which all too easily confirm this ideology. They have always had a 'point of production' bias, seeing factory work as real work and men in overalls as the real workers. They have been slow to adjust to the changing shape of the British economy, slow to recognise the centrality of service work, slow to admit that women's work is just as real as men's.

For women such blindness is a major constraint. It diverts attention from the sectors they dominate and makes us measure the success of the strategy by the number of male jobs it creates in manufacturing. It makes spending on services seem a cost rather than an improvement. Yet so many of the reforms we need to change women's lives involve *more* social services – more public spending on the tasks that women now do for free. The devaluation of service work makes us think of these as a luxury, something we can only indulge in when times are good. It makes 'getting the economy right' the first priority, improving services a secondary concern.

All three criticisms come down to one basic point. The strategy talks of the working class or working people as if this were a single unified mass. By doing that it ends up talking about men. Full employment means jobs for the boys. Popular control means workplace democracy for male trade unionists. Reviving the economy means reviving male-dominated manufacturing. The strategy, of course, says no more about men than it does about women, but given the power structures of our society it does not need to. Unless we discuss explicitly what any strategy means for women, we fall unthinkingly into policies for men.

Would the AES work?

The main counter-argument is that at least the alternative economic strategy would work. The great attraction of the strategy has been its nitty-gritty concern with the here-and-now. Against vague dreams of a socialist millennium, it presents a detailed and forceful programme for short-term change. Against all the complexities of a new and better world, it gives us straightforward policies designed to bring us back to the old. It starts from the things we once had – full employment, economic growth, rising living standards – conditions we used to expect as a right. It then leads us on from these to the argument that in this new era of monopoly power and capitalist crisis, we need radical planning. It avoids the problem of winning support for new demands: it avoids, for example, the daunting task of persuading men to relinquish some of their privileges. It simply builds on existing and widely shared demands, arguing for an alternative strategy as the only way to meet them.

Compared with this, all feminists have to offer is the argument that the strategy needs women if it is to succeed. 'Without widespread support from women,' Judith Hunt has said, 'the alternative economic strategy will remain on people's shelves tidied away in pamphlets and books.' Why should women support a strategy that says so little about their needs and experience? Why should they put their weight behind something that offers them so little?

The truth of the matter may be that an alternative strategy can do perfectly well without women, that they have so little power that their interests can be safely ignored. But we can broaden the question further. Why should *anyone* support a strategy that threatens conflict with capital, unless it promises something new?

Supporters of the strategy tend to present it as more straightforward than it is. With planning, they argue, we can do all those things capital has refused to do: invest in Britain instead of overseas; invest in new machinery instead of soldiering on with the old; raise the productivity of labour instead of cutting wages. But capital had its reasons for refusing to do these things, and will not readily co-operate in what it sees as irrational. Forcing private firms to act against their will is no easy matter.

The AES offers a scenario of conflict, and for what? To create those conditions capitalism used to be reasonably good at providing. Capitalism once delivered the goods, so why not believe those who tell us it will again? Faced with a choice between Tory stringency and the unknown, untried prospects of planning it may well be rational to wait and see. Why take the path of conflict? A radically alternative strategy needs wide support and that means capturing people's imagination with a radically new vision. A strategy that offers something new might get that support. One that promises what we used to get without all this bother is less compelling.

When socialists argue that they can do what capitalism used to do, only better, they are on sticky ground. Within its own terms capitalism is reasonably efficient. It does go through crises, and it always leaves some people in poverty, but as a provider of cars, washing machines and TV sets, it has done a pretty good job. The real argument against capitalism is that it only meets those needs that will make it money.

Capitalism will not, for example, build decent houses for the mass of workers. With the existing technology of house building and current wage levels for workers, capitalism cannot build houses cheaply enough to sell at a profit. So the state has had to step in with massive housing subsidies, building council houses for some and giving huge mortgage subsidies to others. Left to itself, capitalism could not have housed us.

Similarly, capitalism will not build nurseries for our children unless it gets desperate for women workers. If it needed female labour to such an extent that it became worth while to finance nurseries, we might soon have child care for all. But, short of that, capitalism will not bother itself with the needs of mothers or children.

Capitalism cannot guarantee us equality; it cannot meet some of our most basic needs. The fact that it cannot today provide us with jobs is only the tip of the iceberg – yet the alternative economic strategy rests its entire case on this. It makes unemployment the central, almost exclusive problem, and though there is no doubt that this is an overriding problem for many people, we should not therefore abandon our demands for more. Tempting as it is to reduce our demands in the face of crisis, we should resist this pressure. We should be asking how to go forward, not how to get back – and unless we do this, we will never fire people's imagination enough to achieve change.

3.

The Right to Work

If the alternative economic strategy is so inadequate, what should we do instead? For those supporters of the strategy itching to get back to concrete proposals, there are some obvious reforms that spring to mind. Even within the general demand of women's right to work (which, as I shall argue, is a limited demand), there are some immediate priorities for action.

Five points for action

Nurseries
This is such a basic need that it barely needs to be stated. The Employment Protection Act gives women the right to reclaim their old job (or a near substitute) if they go back to work within 29 weeks of the birth of their child. But without adequate child care provision this means very little. It is virtually impossible to get a nursery place for a very young child, unless you are a single parent or the social services consider your child 'at risk'. For the vast majority of women, having a child is incompatible with full-time work. Only about one in twenty married women work full-time when they have a child below school age, and only three in twenty single women in the same position.

Without nurseries, women must either give up their job, find part-time work, or look around for a childminder. Of course, many might prefer to give up their jobs when they have young children, but the way things are at present there is no real choice. The man certainly won't give up work, and neither the state nor the employer will provide a nursery.

Provision for 3- to 5-year-olds is somewhat better, but even here the demand exceeds the supply. Surveys show that four out of five parents with children of this age would like some kind of child care provision. Less than one-third of them get it. Without comprehensive child care facilities, women's right to work remains a farce. So why not make a massive investment programme in nurseries a central plank in any alternative strategy? This would certainly provide jobs (in construction, catering, nursery nursing and teaching) and simultaneously meet a crying need.

Equal pay legislation

Existing legislation should be overhauled. For a start, the Equal Pay Act is too restrictive, applying only where men and women do the same job, a broadly similar one, or one rated as equivalent by job evaluation experts. With current segregation between men's and women's work, this means it has limited application. There are not that many women working alongside men. If the legislation was extended to cover 'equal pay for work of equal value' (which is what EEC directives recommend) we could begin to compare different jobs in different workplaces.

This in itself would be no final solution. As anyone who has been involved in it will know, job evaluation can be an awkward business. Sex stereotypes are written deep into our notions of skill and work is often classified as skilled because men do it, unskilled because it is done by women. Women are supposed to have nimble fingers, so dexterity gets a low value; men are expected to be stronger, so physical effort rates more. Nevertheless, studies show that when women apply for equal pay under job evaluation clauses, they tend to get a better deal. Once we are allowed to extend equal pay to comparisons *between* employers, across the line that divides men's and women's work, we can hope for further improvement.

As well as this, many argue that we should combine the Equal Pay and Sex Discrimination Acts in a single unified body. With two Acts there is a gap in the middle, and part-time workers disappear down it. When hourly rates are lower than they are for full-timers doing the same job – the situation for many part-time women workers – existing legislation offers no way out. Employers cannot be made responsible under the Equal Pay Act, because the difference between full-time and part-time working is treated as a 'genuine material difference'. Neither can employers be pinned under the Sex Discrimination Act, because even when the wages *clearly* discriminate against women (when the women are part-timers, and the men full-timers) this is a pay matter and therefore outside the scope of the Act. Between the two, part-timers get nothing. One of the major sources of women's low pay is left unquestioned.

Parity for part-timers

Part-time workers should get the same rate for the job as full-timers, but also the same rights to employment protection. Under the Employment Protection Act, full-timers have to be a year in the same job before they are protected against unfair dismissal, and 2 years before they get their full maternity and redundancy rights. Part-time workers doing less than 8 hours a week get no such rights, and those working between 8 and 16 hours have to be 5 years in the same job before they qualify. Yet about 6 per cent of women workers are doing less than 8 hours a week, and about 20 per cent are doing between 8 and 16.

These women are highly vulnerable in a crisis. When redundancies are threatened, they are often the first to go; though they may agree on nothing else, both unions and management see these women as the most dispensable. Just take the example of electrical engineering. Between 1974 and 1977, 38,000 unskilled and semi-skilled jobs were lost. Nearly half of these – 18,000 – were part-time jobs done by women.

Of course, on the other side of the coin, employers have reacted to the crisis by getting rid of permanent, protected staff and replacing them by more casual workers. Offices have switched to 'temp' typists – taking them on in peak periods and dropping them when their services are no longer needed. The number of part-time workers has increased. In 1971 only one in three of the women at work were part-time; now it is up to two in five. Shops, for example, have switched to a skeleton staff of full-timers, boosted by part-time or casual workers in peak hours and peak periods. Because the Employment Protection Act distinguishes between full-time and part-time, and between those with long service and those with short service, it acts as an inducement to employers to make their workforce predominantly casual.

The latest stage in this is the government's job-splitting scheme. This was introduced in 1983 as a ploy to reduce unemployment figures. Employers are encouraged to split an existing full-time job into two part-time ones, and paid £750 per job as inducement. Employers' associations were quick to spot the potential. If employers take on two workers at 15 hours each a week, they can get round the Employment Protection Act, escaping any future claims for unfair dismissal, maternity leave or redundancy pay.

As long as part-time work means fewer rights, employers will take advantage of this. So the women who have to work part-time as the only way of coping with child care and other responsibilities end up with less pay and little, if any, job security. Workers should not be penalised for working fewer hours than the norm. Part-time workers need full-time rates and full-time rights.

Positive action at work

At work we should press our employers to adopt an equal opportunities programme. Jobs are still advertised in a way that makes it clear that no women need apply, or in journals that few women read. Employers still claim they cannot take on women because they have no facilities for them – as if building an extra toilet is a multi-million investment. Others compliment themselves on their open-mindedness, but say that women just do not want 'male' jobs.

Employers still penalise women for the years they take out of work to look after children. Sometimes they set age limits so low that most women are too old when they go back to work after bringing up children. In the railways, there is a strict 'break in service' agreement, which means anyone who leaves the job has to return at the very bottom of their grade. In primary schools, women teachers get no credit for their experience as mothers, so if they take time off to have children they end up clustering in the lowest grades. Women lose out in both recruitment and promotion.

One of the major inequalities between men and women is the concentration of women in low-paid, unskilled jobs. Changing this means positive action.

In the USA workers have won massive programmes of positive action. Take the American Telephone and Telegraph Company. In the early 1970s 92.4 per cent of its employees (total workforce = almost one million) were in jobs that were either 90 per cent male or 90 per cent female. After pressure from women's and black groups, the Equal Employment Opportunity Commission (equivalent to the British Equal Opportunity Commission and Commission for Racial Equality combined) took up the case. After three years of legal wrangles, the company agreed to a settlement. It paid the equivalent of £50 million in back pay to women and black employees who had been unfairly treated in the past. It set up a five-year programme for changing the balance, with targets for each of the different jobs in the company. As a result of this programme, women and black people got nearly half the new jobs and promotions that came up during the five-year period.

In the USA, the government sets conditions for any firm that wins a government contract. If it supplies goods or services worth $20,000 or more, the firm has to prove it is giving equal opportunities to women and ethnic minorities. It has to submit reports on the sexual and racial balance of the workforce, and plans for changing this. In Britain, legislation is not so tough and no government has taken similar steps. Few firms have got beyond the rudimentary stage of altering how they advertise jobs.

The existing Sex Discrimination Act makes it illegal to favour women over men at the point of choosing people for a job. If the man and woman are equally qualified, employers can pick the woman – but not if she has fewer qualifications for the job. What they can do is set up training schemes to encourage and equip women for male-dominated jobs. So far, few have acted on this. Yet if we really want women to have the same right to work as men – and mean this to include the same right to good jobs – we need to move in this direction. We need positive action, something more than that wonderful phrase 'we are an equal opportunities employer' tagged on to the end of the job advertisement.

Positive action in training and education

The corollary of this is positive action in schools. Long before we get to the point of looking for jobs we are already set in our stereotyped ways. Schools still teach domestic science to girls and carpentry to boys; they still train girls in typing and commercial skills, boys in mechanical ones; they still encourage girls to study arts subjects, boys science ones.

Sex stereotypes run so deep that it would be a miracle if teachers had escaped. Those responsible for education often need retraining themselves, so part of a positive action programme would be in-service training in the problems of sex discrimination. The school curriculum should be redesigned to eliminate any sexist bias, and the way that boys and girls are recruited for different options should be reviewed.

Recruitment on to training courses should also be monitored, and, where necessary, special courses set up to train women in typically male skills (and, of course, men in typically female ones). Changes here are dauntingly long term. In those few cases where courses have been devised to train women in, say, engineering skills, there are often problems finding enough students. The dead weight of tradition presses hard, but positive action in education and training can at least go some way towards job equality for women.

Responses in the labour movement

On paper at least, the labour movement supports most of these demands. The TUC has its *Charter for the Under-Fives* which calls for full child care provision for any children under five whose parents want it. It has its *Charter for Women at Work*, and a list of recommendations for positive action in jobs and education. The remaining blind spot is over part-time work, but, with this major exception, the labour movement is formally committed to many of these changes.

Officially again, it has admitted the bias towards men in the way full employment is discussed. It is now widely recognised that figures for the registered unemployed understate the number of women who want work. Many married women do not register because they have no right to unemployment benefit; many women with young children are told they cannot register because, with the children, they are not really 'available for work'. When people now estimate the number of jobs needed for full employment, they add in some figure for these invisible women.

In their book on *The Alternative Economic Strategy* the CSE London Working Group added on an extra half million to cover these hidden hands. *Labour Research*, in December 1982, took this even further, adding in yet another half million for the women who *would* have been looking for work if it were not for the crisis. As the article pointed out, women's employment was rising at the rate of 1 per cent each year through the 1970s, and if this trend had continued there would be even more women looking for jobs. 'An even more radical assumption,' the article continued, 'would be that women should expect to work as much as men – this would add a further 25 per cent of women, or 4,000,000 more women kept out of work.'

Changes in how unemployment is counted reflect a wider acceptance of women's right to work. The 1982 Labour Party Programme declares that 'the achievement of equal rights will be central to our economic strategy'. It attacks the out-moded notion that man is the breadwinner, and defines full employment as jobs for all who want them. It outlines a programme for more child care provision (though only for children over three years old) and discusses (without reaching any final conclusion) ways of equalising tax and social security.

Such proposals mark important shifts, though few women would put too much faith in them. Paper commitments can so easily reflect the dedication of those who drafted the documents, and the apathy of the rest. Programmes are not mani-

festos, and manifestos rarely end up as government policy.
Women's equality will not be won in committee rooms alone.

Who wants the right to work anyway?

There is a more fundamental problem. At the risk of sounding
grudging, these fine words are too old-fashioned. They deal
with *women's right to work*, on equal terms and with equal
pay to men. Yet many feminists have questioned this slogan,
saying the problem for women is too much work rather than
too little.

Equal access to the male world of work is not good enough.
For many people, work has no intrinsic interest. Yet the lives
of men are dictated by their jobs, with many working night
shifts, 35 per cent working overtime, and few finding time to
see their children. Do we really want women subjected to similar constraints? And when women do get equal access to paid
work, who will do the housework and look after the children?
As many women have discovered in the last 30 years, the
answer is them. They find themselves doing two jobs instead of
one.

Yet more jobs for women has been the classic solution to
their oppression. From the nineteenth century onwards, socialists and feminists alike have argued for getting women out of
the home and into the workforce. Once released from the isolation and drudgery of housework, once drawn into the com-
radeship of work, women would find themselves on an equal
footing with men. This was why Marx and Engels saw capitalism as liberating for women. With all its brutalities, at least it
dragged them out into the open and exploited them equally
with men. Under socialism, this would become the basis for
genuine freedom, as men and women shared together in social
production to meet their needs.

Child care and housework, in this argument, would simply
be socialised. There would be canteens at school and work
instead of food preparation inside every home; nurseries
instead of women enslaved to child care; house-cleaning services instead of today's individualised sweeping and dusting.

'Public dining-rooms, crèches, kindergartens,' these, proclaimed Lenin, are 'the simple everyday means . . . which can
in fact emancipate women'. No more private drudgery, but a
rational allocation of social resources.

It is in many ways an appealing vision. Housework is a deadening experience, a monotony of repetition with only the occa-
sional thanks. Many of us would echo the frustration Rebecca
West expressed 70 years ago: 'For heaven's sake, let us take
this unpleasant task and give it over to the specialist to organise
as a trade process.' Looking after children in isolation is not
ideal: children get too little stimulation and the mothers too
much strain. Women *are* happier when they go out to work –
at least if the figures for depression among housewives tell us
anything.

But notice that it is a solution that demands nothing of men.
'Women are oppressed by domestic labour? Let's socialise it
then.' There is no suggestion that men might take their turn.
It is like when you ask a man to help you with the washing-up
and he goes out and buys a dish-washer. Nothing wrong with
dish-washers (except that they are enormously wasteful of
energy!) but it does raise a few niggling doubts. When socialisation is presented as an alternative to shared labour, it blocks
discussion of men's role. In the Soviet Union and much of
Eastern Europe child care has been significantly socialised, but
it is women who staff the nurseries and women who care for
the children after hours.

As far as children are concerned, there are limits to socialisation. Children (like anyone else) object to long hours in institutions, and even the best nursery could only cover part of their
day. Child care is a 24-hour business and demands a 24-hour
solution.

For many feminists the ideal is collective living. Instead of
the nuclear family, we could have a group of people – men and
women, parents and non-parents, adults, teenagers and children – who would share together the household tasks. But here
we face a short-term/long-term dilemma. Experiments in collective living have often been fragile, generating acute resent-
ments before dissolving into more conventional family

patterns. It is not easy to find a new way of life when all of us share the insecurities and expectations of the old. Children bring their own dynamic, and households that achieve a stable balance between parents and non-parents are few and far between. Whatever our hopes for the future, we cannot rely on collective living as a solution for today.

For the present, most children are brought up in households with a father and a mother, and the task of caring for them falls on the mother. As Anna Coote has argued in *New Socialist*, this not only confines women by its relentless demands, but also limits the development of the men and children:

> Cared for almost exclusively by women, children grow up with a limited picture of the respective characters and capacities of males and females: this is one of the main ways in which sex stereotypes become rooted in people's minds. While men continue to segregate themselves from children, they are cut off from a range of experience which would broaden their understanding and no doubt alter their political priorities (and which they might even enjoy). It scarcely needs to be added that while women bear the full responsibility for child care, they are forced into economic dependence, subjected to considerable stress and deprived of the opportunity to explore their full potential.

Nurseries can only play a small part in changing such conditions. We also have to change the pattern of child care within each household.

This means a lot more than the right to work. We want equality at home as well as at work. We want jobs that can admit our lives outside, jobs that acknowledge us as people. We want not so much the equal right to work, as the right to a different kind of work.

The right to work less

This is why some feminists have made shorter working hours the crucial issue. They have called for a 30-hour week for all, seeing this as a basis for equal work in the home. We cannot change the sexual division of labour by breeding a race of superwomen. It is not enough simply to equip ourselves to compete better with men, free ourselves from the encumbrances of children, train ourselves in what used to be male skills. The greatest success here will still be capitulation, submission to a world that has no time for us. We have to make work more malleable to human needs. With a maximum of 30 hours for all we could expect everyone to take their share of child care and housework. No guarantee of course – male resistance to women's work will die hard – but at least a chance. A 30-hour week would blur the distinction between full-time and part-time; undermine the still powerful notion that men are breadwinners, women dependants; and free men to spend more time with their children. It could be the basis of a far-reaching assault on capitalist work as we know it.

So is it to be the right to work or the right to a different kind of work? The question harks back to a recurrent debate within the women's movement. Through two centuries of feminist thinking there has been a tension between fighting for access to the man's world and fighting for recognition of the women's. Some women have relentlessly denied any difference between the sexes, insisting on women's right to do anything that is done by men. Others have gloried in the difference, staking a claim for the special needs and experience of women. Some have fought against male privileges, and concentrated on a woman's right to vote, to education, to work in the professions. Others have focused on issues related to motherhood, leading campaigns against child poverty, or resisting military adventurism.

Male socialists have usually found the first approach more sympathetic. The world of work is what they know best, and they can understand women's discontent at being left out of this. Equality defined as women's right to work is something they can feel at home with. They are ill at ease in a world of female concerns. Equality as a greater commitment to children is not so appealing – a less 'political' demand. Not surprisingly, men find less attraction in the idea of fitting work around children.

Women, too, have found this a dilemma. Many of those active in politics through the twentieth century have shied away from 'women's issues', knowing only too well that matters of motherhood or children are treated as marginal affairs. Any woman who allowed herself to be identified with such issues was on a sure line to oblivion. But perhaps because women have now tasted the delights of waged work and found them wanting, perhaps because work itself is such a routinised and uninspiring performance, many have now rebelled. Since the revival of the women's movement in the late 1960s, women have been adamant that they want a different world. Not just equal rights to the same old world, but something better and different. The issue of working hours has become one of the cornerstones of this demand, and I shall devote the next chapter to it.

4.

The Time to Live

What do I do all day? Well, starting from eight o'clock in the morning, we work in here right up till five o'clock – well, we do when we've got work. Then I'm into shops, running in and out for my messages. Then by the time I've got them all fed and washed there's all my housework to start. I'm lucky if I get sat down by ten o'clock, then a few hours' sleep, and back down here again in the morning.

As this machinist in a Scottish clothing factory makes clear, women often work grotesque hours. At whatever stage in their lives you catch them, the picture is much the same. When the children are young, the day seems endless. They get a bit older, and most women return to work, picking up a part-time job, or, like this woman, a full 8 to 5 day. But however long the hours on the job, there is always the housework and always the child care. Endless activity, then the children leave home – and for many women too much work turns into too little. Adult lives are swallowed up by work, then suddenly there's an empty space.

On the other side of the coin things also look bleak. Men in Britain work extraordinarily long hours in their jobs, and, like women, they work longest while their children are young. Half of all male manual workers do overtime, averaging 10 hours each a week. Workers have fought for over a century to cut working hours – today's May Day celebrations go back as far as 1886, when workers demonstrated for an 8-hour day. Yet in Britain, the 40-hour week is still a distant dream.

In those areas where overtime hours are worst – in the baking industry, on the railways, in the post office – some are working 60 hours or more. For many, systematic overtime is just part of the job. The hours are not only long, they are also unsocial. One-quarter of male manual workers do shiftwork – maybe a permanent night shift, maybe alternating days and nights over a two-week period, maybe the notorious swing shift where they rotate endlessly between three shifts.

Hours like these make men slaves to their jobs. Life becomes a monotonous circuit of work, sleep, spend the wages, then back to work again. Leisure can be no more demanding than watching TV and going for a drink – anything else is just too much effort. In a recent survey of unskilled male workers, 90 per cent of the married ones rated a 'good family life' as more important than enjoyment of their job. But the fact is they may end up with neither. Fathers see little of their children – with the usual bitter twist, they work most overtime when their children are young. Basic wages are low, and overtime or shiftwork often become the only way to make a living. Adult lives are consumed by work, then overtime slackens, retirement begins, and people are left to fill that gap.

Capitalism seemed to promise us a fixed working day with freedom to do as we wanted outside. This never meant much to women, and with hours like these it does not mean much to men either. Long hours might be bearable if the job itself was interesting, but when the skill and challenge has been taken from work, it ends up as drudgery. Work dictates our lives, yet offers us little stimulation.

Work as it might be

Forget for the moment how things are and think about how they might be. What, in the long term, do we want from our work? What kind of changes would we like to see, and which priorities should we set ourselves?

Traditionally, socialists have divided over work. Marx often talked of work as what makes us human, and looked forward to a future where we would develop ourselves in work. One of the absurdities of capitalism, he argued, is that it makes work so unpleasant that we shun it like the plague. We feel we are only living outside of work, and we escape as soon as we can to the privacies of leisure.

Yet freed from the narrowing constraints of profit, which tie us like automata to one soul-destroying task for life, we could turn work into creative activity. For the present we are defined and limited by it. Our capacities are stunted and our skills denied. But imagine a world where we could move freely from one task to another. As Marx put it in one of his wilder moments, we could 'hunt in the morning, fish in the afternoon, rear cattle in the evening, criticise after dinner'. No more a routine of deadening monotony, but a constantly changing pattern of chosen and challenging work. We could break down the destructive division between mental and manual labour, which condemns so many of us to mindless tasks; we could make all jobs a source of interest and pleasure.

More sceptical socialists have dismissed this as a romantic dream. They argue that work under any guise is always a drag. In another mood, Marx himself described it as a 'realm of necessity' which we should cut to its minimum to make ourselves free. In any society we have to work, and in a socialist society we can try to make this as pleasant as possible. But the truth is that work is an intrusion, that real freedom begins only where work ends. 'The shortening of the working day,' as Marx once said, 'is its basic prerequisite.' Freedom is freedom *from* work, and our priority should be to cut the hours we waste in it.

Today, this debate is yet more poignant. In the advanced capitalist countries work has become so monotonous and fragmented that even employers have expressed concern. Assembly-line techniques have taken the skill out of labour, pushing many workers to their limit. Indifference, absenteeism, even sabotage, are the result. Pride in one's work has become largely anachronistic. The ship-builders who cheered when 'their' ship was launched are increasingly figures from history – and not only because so few ships are now launched from Britain. Few workers now identify with the product of their labour. The job is just a job and the point of doing it is the pay. For many people, work is just a bore.

Today, as in Marx's time, there are two main responses. We can say that work is always oppressive, and try to reduce it. We can say the work could be better, and try to improve it.

Rudolf Bahro and André Gorz

Take two recent contributions to the discussion: Rudolf Bahro's *The Alternative in Eastern Europe* and André Gorz's *Farewell to the Working Class*.

Gorz is pessimistic about changing work. He accepts that some kind of socialised production is necessary (imagine making a video-machine in your own back garden) but argues that this kind of work will always be standardised and never determined by ourselves. Nothing can bring back the craft-pride of the past. But new technology gives us a chance to cut work. Instead of 40, 50, or even 60 hours a week, we could do just 20 – with our real energies devoted to our life outside. He envisages us in a kind of glorified do-it-yourself utopia:

> Repair and do-it-yourself workshops in blocks of flats, neighbourhood centres or rural communities should enable everyone to make or invent things as they wish. Similarly, libraries, places to make music or movies, 'free' radio and television stations, open spaces for communication, circulation and exchange, and so on, need to be accessible to everyone.

It may seem an odd dream, but it comes from a real problem. If we think that being creative is part of what makes us human *and* we believe that today's jobs destroy that faculty, this is one possible way out.

Bahro wants us to concentrate on changing the jobs themselves. He sees leisure activities, 'hobbies', as at best compensation. As long as the hours at work deaden our lives, we have no hope of development outside. Workers have already wrested more leisure time from capital (though British workers have been less successful than others) but few would claim that this has made us more creative. While our hours on the job are so dense and yet so barren, we cannot begin to use our free time. What we need, he argues, is a new kind of work. Unskilled jobs should be abolished, and work reorganised so that each worker shares in both unskilled and skilled activities. Time pressures should be reduced so that workers have space to think for themselves. We should organise work so that it allows human development; not sacrifice this development to the demands of efficiency.

But then the price of this may be longer hours at work. The kind of 'time-wasting' deplored by managers is, Bahro claims, crucial to our creativity. We need time to experiment on our machines and computers, time to call meetings as and when problems arise. We need a working day with some slack built in, a working day less 'efficient' than before. The implication may be the same old working hours: a 40-hour week in which we 'really work' for only 30.

Both writers seem a long way from today's crisis. Bahro is drawing on the experience of East Germany, and proposing an alternative for countries that have already introduced central planning. Gorz is drawing on his experience of France, but has little time for the issues that obsess French socialists today. Compared with the alternative economic strategy, both writers are looking a long way ahead. But their utopianism echoes the thoughts of many socialist feminists. They are questioning the exclusive emphasis on wages and jobs; they are saying we must look again at the nature of work.

So far, neither has taken full account of the experience of women. Bahro has little to say about them. He simply ignores the relationship between hours on the job and hours at home, forgetting that more time at work means more rushing around to fit in the shopping, the cleaning and the children. His strategy is effectively for male workers.

Gorz comes closer to these problems, and refers extensively to the unwaged work at home. The difficulty is that he tends to a romanticised version that few houswives could confirm. 'Women's activities and qualities,' he says, 'prefigure a post-capitalist and post-industrial society.' Because women live so much of their lives outside the competitive, productivist world of the (male) economy, they aleady work in a more creative way. The aim of the women's movement, he argues, should be to extend this non-economic rationality further.

More work, not less, should be done in the local community. Medical care, for example, could be brought back to the home. We could have high-technology hospitals for certain complaints, and treat the rest in the home and local community. Instead of relying on institutions to care for the young, the sick and the elderly, we could reclaim the time to care for them ourselves.

For women this sounds a rather chilling note. The more labour that is done in the home, the more likely it is that women will do it. We have good reason to suspect proposals for diverting tasks to the home and local community – too often this is a euphemism for more work for women. Gorz shows little understanding of the tensions inside the family. He grossly overstates the extent to which domestic labour is already shared. 'Taking care of babies is no longer exclusively allocated to women,' he claims, 'wage labour no longer seems more "noble" or admirable than unpaid autonomous activity within the extended or nuclear family.' Most women will wonder who he has been talking to. We can build on Gorz's ideas, but we must first adapt them to the realities of sexual division.

A feminist strategy on hours

The problems raised in this debate are important to all of us, but they have to be reshaped to suit the needs of women. Bahro is right when he points to the horrors of work, and I share his commitment to making work better. But the routines of domestic drudgery can be as devastating as those of factory life – as one slogan has it, 'housework is a worm eating away at one's ideas'. Attacking the monotony of work should mean attacking *all* work, and that implies equalising and transforming the work that goes on in the home.

Gorz is right when he questions the simple solution of more

jobs, more institutions, more socialised production. Getting women into the offices and factories has not solved their problems; putting babies into nurseries and old people into homes is not our ideal. But how are women to free themselves from the demands on their time? The hours they spend at work are often the least of their problems. It is the burden of work in the home that looms largest.

The key approach for women is to treat all work as a whole, to recognise that work goes on both inside and outside the home, and to develop a strategy that can cope with it all. One of the most dehumanising aspects of work today is that it does not acknowledge our needs as people. Men are expected to turn up for overtime, and no one asks where their children are or how their daily needs are met. Times of work are set to suit the employers – no firm employing men considers the times of the schools or the closing hours of the shops. It is accepted as normal that people work twice as hard when they have children – no one suggests that this is precisely when they need most time off. Work is organised as if every worker (whether man or woman) has a full-time housewife at home. This is what we have to challenge.

A priority in this area is to reduce men's hours at work. At the moment women are silenced by male overtime and shift-work. The hours on the job seem to excuse men from domestic tasks – after all those hours on the night shift, surely they have earned their rest? The excuse wears thin as more and more women go out to work. But when it comes down to it, a man back from work will expect to be waited on, while a woman back from work is supposed to fix a meal and put the kids to bed. On any strict calculation of hours these women may be working longer than the most overworked man. Centuries of male privilege block such simple arithmetic.

Shorter hours at work can begin to challenge this, but only if the change is informed by feminist demands. Men may organise around the relatively simple slogan of shorter hours, but women know the problem is more complex. If, for example, we get a shorter working week at the expense of harder work, the gains will be limited. From their vantage-point in the home, women are well placed to judge. If the man who used to work 50 hours comes home equally exhausted from 30, there will be no change on the domestic front. If men buy their leisure at the price of shorter meal breaks and speed-ups on the line, this will make no difference to the sexual division of labour. We can measure the success of the hours strategy by the *change* it allows at home.

Then there is the question of how shorter hours should be distributed. When men talk of cutting hours they dream of the 3-day weekend. But we cannot package children and housework into a 3-day week affair. We need an hours strategy that admits the needs of children, which means not just shorter but more flexible hours, and a working pattern that acknowledges the times of nurseries and schools.

Ambitious as this is, it may seem less so than those wonderful dreams about making work better. The emphasis is more on sharing the work, taking it as it is and making it equal. Is this simply sharing the drudgery, and nothing more progressive than that?

In the long term, I see much wider implications. For a start, once men find themselves with an equal share of housework we shall see countless schemes for making it better! As long as women do it no one cares how it is done, how time-consuming or how isolated it is. Bringing it out in to the open will begin to change this.

Second, employers will be forced to recognise their workers as people, something that goes against the grain in today's society. At present we are supposed to lead a double life: at work under the employer's commands, and at home under our (or is it his?) own. We can stop this schizophrenia. If jobs do not fit with the rest of our lives, we can begin to refuse them. Cutting working hours is shorthand for something much more: a world dedicated to human beings, instead of one that sacrifices us to profit.

Trade unions and time

Shorter hours has re-emerged as a trade union concern, and

there is now a European *and* British campaign for reduced working time. The main impetus is unemployment. As the crisis deepens, trade unionists have begun to question the absurdity of millions out of work and millions more with too much to do. And as the potential of the new micro-computer technology unveils itself, many begin to wonder whether we shall ever see full employment again. It seems a good moment for radical reductions in working hours.

In 1979 the European TUC adopted a programme of action, aiming for a 35-hour week and 6 weeks' paid holiday each year. On both scores, British workers lag far behind. In comparison with other European workers, they get much shorter paid holidays each year and much longer overtime hours each week (see Table 3).

Table 3   **Working hours in Europe, 1977**

	Manual workers doing 45 hours or more (%)	Manual workers doing 48 hours or more (%)
UK	28.8	20.2
France	25.5	8.6
Italy	13.1	9.9
West Germany	11.1	6.3
Luxemburg	9.0	6.8
Netherlands	6.4	4.4
Denmark	4.5	2.8
Belgium	3.9	2.8

The British situation is unusual in two ways. First, the actual hours worked are very high. Second, there is a marked contrast between the hours of manual and non-manual workers. The latter are more likely to have a basic week of 37 or 38 hours, and much less likely to work overtime. In the rest of Europe there is not such a sharp distinction.

The British TUC has had some success with its campaign. By 1981, more than half the full-time workforce could boast a basic week of 38 hours or less. The engineering industry now has a 39-hour week, as does the construction industry. Printers have used negotiations over new technology to push for even greater reductions, with targets of 32, 30 and even 24 hours per week.

Overtime hours have not, however, changed much. The crisis has made some difference, and the total number of manual workers doing overtime has dropped from 60 per cent in the mid-1970s to its present level of around 50 per cent. But the hours these workers do stay much the same. Ten hours a week on top of the basic remains the norm.

Progress reports from the TUC campaign make depressing reading. Successive reductions in the *basic* week have done little to total hours, and, worst of all, the reports say nothing about women. The campaign is really about male working hours – most women already do 38 hours or less in their paid work. The idea that shorter hours might change domestic labour rarely surfaces, and no one seems to be thinking of the campaign as anything more than a campaign for more leisure and more jobs.

When they discuss how workers should take the extra hours, the reports address a male audience – looking forward to the 3-day weekend, rather than shorter hours each day. Yet this is something on which men and women have very different views. When Sweden brought in shorter hours for parents, the government did a survey to work out how best to arrange these hours. Men wanted a shorter working week; women a shorter working day. Men wanted more leisure time (for playing with the children?); women wanted freedom to leave work early and pick up the children from nursery or school. In this case the women won out, and parents now have the option of working a 6-hour day.

In the British campaign, the sole gesture towards this comes in the checklist for union negotiators, which points out that more flexible daily hours could help 'people with family commitments'. Against this is the more appealing idea of taking the extra time in a single block, so releasing workers for 'leisure and educational purposes'. Reading between the lines, the message is this: if the workforce is predominantly female, shop stewards might try for a shorter working day; if it is male, they should go for the longer weekend.

In most of the recent agreements workers have opted for going home early on Friday. With pathetic reductions of 1 or 2 hours this may make sense – spread over 5 days the gain would become invisible. But what if the campaign gathers momentum and more substantial reductions are won? Time off on Fridays will not change much in the home. The potential for challenging sex roles will be lost.

Peering through the fog of current propaganda – with its dire warnings of new technology and its meaningless pronouncements on the joys of leisure – it does seem possible to win shorter working hours. But on present form this will be through intensifying work. Trade unions have so far accepted that any reduction must be 'no cost'. Shorter hours have been financed through higher productivity, which in most cases has taken the crudest form of cutting tea breaks and increasing the speed of work.

As long as this is the approach, employers may show some sympathy. After all, few workers work in all their time on the job, and shorter hours would wonderfully concentrate the mind on reducing 'time-wasting'. With some luck and a bit of imagination, firms could squeeze as much out of the 35-hour week as they now get from the 40-hour one.

Shorter hours can be traded off against harder work, but if they are it will do nothing for women. We need genuine relief from the pressures of waged work, not just fiddling around with the times. Otherwise men will still claim they are too tired to help out around the home; women – with their usual excess of generosity – will probably agree.

Current negotiations leave much to be desired. The concerns of parents have been ignored. The extra hours have been bought at too high a price. Shorter basic hours have not yet dented overtime. That unions take up the issue of hours is a major breakthrough, but so far the needs of women have been ignored. The campaign has been less far-reaching than TUC reports sometimes imply.

Tackling overtime

When women talk of cutting working hours, they have set a more ambitious goal. They call not for 35, but for 30 hours – and even in some cases for 20. The precise figure is perhaps arbitrary. But it has to be large enough to suggest a revolution in domestic work, and realistic enough to convince people we are serious. If the point is sexual equality, then the odd hour here or there will make little difference.

The real crunch is what to do about overtime. With a stretch of imagination we can envisage reasonable basic hours. But what about the overtime? Britain remains one of the few countries in Europe without restrictions on total hours. As *Labour Research* commented in 1981; 'It would be illegal to work the hours currently tolerated in the UK baking and railway industries in almost every other West European country.' Statutory restrictions on male working time have been anathema to many British trade unionists (though statutory restrictions on women are widely supported).

Today, the main legal controls are on child and female labour, a legacy from the Factory Acts of the nineteenth century. Basically, these cover women factory workers, setting limits for the hours and times of their work. They are not supposed to start work before 7.00 a.m., or finish later than 8.00 p.m. They are not supposed to do more than a 9-hour day if they work 6 days a week, or more than 10 hours a day if they work a 5-day week. They are supposed to have a meal break (unpaid) every four and a half hours. The legislation covers manual workers only, and since exemption orders are freely given, in practice only affects about two-thirds of these. The Equal Opportunities Commission has attacked these restrictions as discriminatory against women; the TUC has defended them.

I favour keeping such restrictions. They do keep women out of better-paid shiftwork – but who wants more people subjected to the horrors of shiftwork and the slavery of overtime? The real question is how to extend them to men. Other European countries set limits on male overtime in Norway and

Sweden most night work is illegal for women *and* men. In Britain there is more of a double standard – we applaud restrictions for women but reject them for men.

Attitudes are beginning to change, and overtime working is now getting a bad name. It has been denounced by the TUC as 'stolen time', the 'continuing curse of British industrial life'. The TUC has passed a series of motions about reducing overtime working, and, bit by bit, this has permeated down to the level of local negotiation.

The test is whether the labour movement will seriously consider statutory controls. The traditions of free collective bargaining make this a sticky issue – unions in Britain usually object to government controls, preferring to pursue their claims in their own way. These traditions have long been a problem for women and the issue is important enough to deserve a chapter in itself (see Chapter 6). On the question of hours the signs may seem hopeful, and unions are currently discussing the pros and cons of legislation. But we should not rely too much on this. Unions are still ambivalent towards overtime, and today's mild 'opposition' could well dissolve in a time of economic growth. If we want radical changes we have an uphill struggle ahead.

Legislation is, of course, limited if it leaves the cause of overtime untouched. The key culprit is the sexual division of labour. Basic rates are low in Britain, so many workers rely on overtime or shift pay to make up their wages. But basic rates for women are even lower and no one expects them to work a 50- or 60-hour week. It is the family wage that makes men slaves to overtime. They are still supposed to be the breadwinners, earning enough to support a wife and children. In Chapter 5 I look at what this family-wage model has done to women; in the appalling figures for male overtime we see something of what it has done to men. We need a different system of child support, and financial independence for women – then we could release some of the pressures on male working hours. Chapter 5 looks at possible initiatives in this direction.

Towards equality in the home

Sceptics have pointed out that reductions in working hours offer no guarantee of equality in the home. Printers, for example, now enjoy much shorter hours but we hear little of subsequent domestic upheaval. Shorter hours for men may strengthen women in their battles for domestic equality, but cannot dictate what goes on at home.

This is true enough, and one reaction has been to press for more radical reductions. Even a 6-hour day is hard to combine with a baby – why not a 5-hour day, or even 4? Some of this is just raising the stakes. Trade unions call for a 35-hour week; feminists respond with 30. Trade unionists begin to mumble about $32\frac{1}{2}$; feminists call their bluff with 20. But there is a serious issue here. We need dramatic changes in male working hours if we are to push home the point about men's domestic responsibilities. A few extra hours will make no difference.

I favour the demand for a 30-hour week because it looks feasible. There are things we need and it takes time to produce them. With possibly five million people itching for jobs, we have considerable scope for raising output. But even so, *halving* average working hours would have to mean lower wages. Productivity would have to increase in miraculous ways to offset such a reduction in hours – and while this may be possible over a period, it is unlikely to happen within five or even ten years. We can cut working hours quite considerably without cutting output – economists estimate that a 10 per cent cut in hours would mean only a 3 to 4 per cent loss of output – but beyond a certain point there is a trade-off between hours and income. Feminists have argued that equality means lower wages for some men (more of this in Chapter 6), but few want shorter hours at the expense of already inadequate living standards.

But if 30 hours is the most we can hope for in the immediate future, how do we get men to do the domestic work? Ultimately, no policy can guarantee this. We cannot legislate sexual equality; we can only open up spaces in which women can fight. In the end, it is a matter of daily struggles, some visible, some hidden, some at home, some at work. There is no magic formula for freeing women 'from above'.

If we cast around for policies, the only obvious candidate is shorter hours *for parents*. We could demand shorter hours for all, but even shorter ones for parents – thus making a direct connection between hours saved at work and hours spent at home. This has been the approach in Sweden, where parents have the option of a 6-hour day. But there shorter hours mean less pay, and few can afford to take it up. If we wanted to take this further we could demand a 6-hour day with 8-hour wages, the extra being made up by the state. With this kind of parental right, men might take a new interest in their children.

Clearly, this would mean a redistribution of hours and income – those without children subsidising those who have them. Everyone would be taxed to finance free time for parents. It is a principle we already apply to child benefits, to health care, to education. No one expects those with school-age children to foot the entire bill.

As with any policy, it is hard to be fair to everyone. A straight 30-hour week would treat us all equally – but as a result would give no extra aid to those with children. A 30-hour week for parents would take from one group and give to another – we can imagine the complaints of those who have chosen not to have children.

Deciding the level of the subsidy would be difficult. If parents worked less and got the normal rate for their job, we would be subsidising higher-paid workers more than lower-paid. The printer would get more out of the scheme than the hospital porter. But if we paid the subsidy at the *average* hourly rate for all workers, the higher-paid male workers would be less inclined to take up the option. We would find the familiar pattern of mothers working shorter hours, but not fathers.

Despite the difficulties, the proposal has its attractions. It makes it clear that children are a social responsibility, and lets men know that their shorter hours at work involve longer hours at home. But it does put everything on children, when the work women do in the home is only partly related to child care. And it is, in the end, a very individual solution to bringing up children – making sure the biological parents have more free time, and leaving everyone else to get on with their lives. We need more discussion before we shall find the ideal strategy.

Half a job is better than none?

Another uncertainty is over part-time jobs. Some feminists have argued for more part-time work for women. As long as they have responsibility for housework and child care, women have to take part-time jobs – yet at present only the worst jobs are available part-time. So why not open all jobs to part-time working? Why not make it easier for women to move from full-time hours to part-time, then back again?

More part-time jobs is not a popular slogan when capital has done so much to deprive us of full-time working. The Tory government's job-splitting scheme has met with a hostile reaction from trade unionists, and, given its nature, this is no surprise. It means workers with full-time jobs can be forced into half-time working; and those in the dole queue can be pushed into part-time jobs when what they want is a full-time job. Those who actually want a half-time job – mothers with young children – are excluded from the scheme: employers will only get their £750 bribe if they take workers from the dole queue, and few of these women will be registered as unemployed. As *New Ways to Work* puts it, 'Job-splitting is a way of making people who want full-time work take part-time jobs. People who need part-time work won't be working at all.'

We could, of course, oppose part-time working. We could argue that while workers divide into men with full-time jobs and women with part-time, the latter will always come off worst. They will be stuck in low-paid ghettos, and expected to shoulder all the work in the home. Men will earn the bread, women the extras. Men will take their place in the world of work while women are left holding the babies. Part-time jobs solve problems at women's expense, letting men neatly off the hook. If we are serious about shorter hours for men and equal shares in domestic work, we should perhaps call for *less* part-time work, not more.

But this would be impossibly draconian in Britain, where so many women rely on working part-time. More realistically, we should aim at convergence between full-time and part-time working, approaching this from both ends. Shorter hours for full-timers; better conditions for part-timers. Full-time working as a realistic option for women; part-time working as a realistic option for men.

In the long term, we will always want the possibility of part-time jobs. Even with shorter average hours there will be times when we want to do less than the norm: when studying, perhaps; while bringing up young children; as we get older; or just because we want to. The problem with part-time work is that it is the worst-paid, most insecure, and typically identified with women. We need better conditions, and part-time working as an option for men.

One route to this is job-sharing. Two people divide what used to be a full-time job between them, getting half the hours, half the wages, half the holiday pay, but *all* the security. The main advantage is that it can open up better jobs to those who work part-time. In principle, *any* job could be advertised as one full-time or two job-shares. The extra costs to the employer are minimal, and certainly do not add up to the £750 bribe of the job-splitting scheme.

In practice, this approach has been mainly restricted to the public sector and voluntary organisations. Lothian Health Board has had job-sharers for a number of years; some local authorities are now adopting policies on job-sharing; a number of law centres and community centres have people working on this basis.

Capital, of course, dreams up its own versions of job-sharing and these can be pretty horrific. A West German employers' association recently drafted its own model agreement which would have realised an employer's paradise. Each worker would have to cover for the other in holidays or illness, switching suddenly to full-time working as and when required. The employers would solve their problems of absenteeism, but those workers who chose a job-share as a way to cope with other demands would find themselves in an impossible situation. Agreements like these are a caricature of job-sharing, as is the British initiative of job-splitting.

But the basic idea is a good one. Fundamentally, what it means is this: part-time workers should be seen as doing exactly the same jobs as full-timers, the only difference being that they get less pay. We should not have ghettos of part-time jobs and full-time jobs, but people working different hours in every job. Working less than the norm should not condemn us to the least-skilled, lowest-paid work.

The real challenge is extending this to men. That means, first, introducing the idea into jobs that are typically male: not only office jobs, but factory jobs; not only the public sector, but the private. Second, it means some guarantee that a worker on part-time hours can go back to full-time when desired. At present virtually no man would choose to work part-time when his children are young, partly because he expects the mother to do this, but partly because he cannot afford to lose his own higher-paid job. In the long term, anyone should be able to drop to part-time hours with a guarantee of full-time work when he or she desires. Before seeking this long-term guarantee, we could make some short-term demands. We can demand that all parents have the option of half-time working for up to 2 years after a child is born; they could then reclaim their old job on full-time terms. This would, of course, inconvenience the employer – but not as much as present arrangements inconvenience us.

Changing the pattern of work

The final issue is the actual pattern of work – not the hours we work but the times. Employers have long recognised *women's* domestic duties when they set the times of work: many women work a 10 a.m. to 3 p.m. shift, or the romantically named 'dawn' or 'twilight' shifts. Employers do not make the same adjustments for men.

We have to build the needs of parents into the working day, not just for women but for men, too. Negotiations over hours and shifts should always take this into account, not only when the workforce is female. We should not, for example, expect people with young children to do nightwork. Say 'women with young children' and everyone will agree (conveniently forgetting that army of night cleaners, many of whom have young children). But say 'men with young children' and it seems an impossible demand. Yet nightwork, like anything else, is an arena of struggle. When employers invest in new machines, of course they want to keep them going all hours – but why should workers co-operate with this? If we objected to men on the nightshift as strongly as we object to women, we would resist these pressures.

We need different shifts, but also flexibility for the emergencies that dog our lives. This means the right to time off, not just more flexible hours. In the 1970s the panacea was 'flexitime', introduced into many offices for their largely female workers. With flexitime, the workers agree a core period when all are at work, then fit in extra hours as and when they suit – sometimes coming in early, sometimes working late, sometimes working through meal breaks. It was hailed as a great advance for women, and even more for employers. 'The greatest advance in management and labour relations for many years,' proclaimed one glossy brochure – produced by a company that sold the necessary clocking-in equipment.

It began as a way of dealing with traffic jams: too many workers were losing too much time in the rush hour. With flexitime they are expected to make up lost hours. If they get in late they must work late to cover, and as a result some found themselves working longer hours than before. Where the employer used to turn a blind eye, the machine now registers the moment of arrival to the nearest second. Where employers once gave workers time off for the dentist, the doctor, Christmas shopping, with flexitime they have to make their own arrangements. The 'free' time once taken as part of the job has gone.

Of course, many women welcomed it – it helped that delicate balancing act between work and home. But it still left *them* with this problem, releasing not only the men but the employer, too. Flexible hours are desirable, but at present they can work in the opposite direction to the one I am proposing. They can strengthen the convention that private life must not interfere with work. Instead of making employers accountable for our needs outside, flexitime can provide the perfect excuse for ignoring these needs. The responsibility is put firmly back with the women.

At present, flexible hours apply to typically female jobs, and there are difficulties in extending them to the typically male. You cannot have flexitime for assembly-line workers. The work relies on everyone in place at the same time. You cannot have flexitime for refuse collection. The work has to wait until the whole team turns up. Flexible hours may have limited application.

One alternative is to give people the right to paid time off. When a child falls ill, has to go to the doctor or dentist, cannot attend the nursery because of a flu epidemic, when any of these daily emergencies arise parents should get paid leave. In Sweden, anyone with children under 12 years old can take sick leave for up to 60 days each year. In Britain it is just assumed that the women will pick up the pieces. 'Private life' is not to interfere with work, and most definitely not with *men's work*. It is about time we stopped this. People have lives outside of work, and work should adapt itself accordingly. If we can give people paid sick leave for their own illness, we can give it to them for the illness of their children.

Who pays?

All the proposals go against current criteria of profitability. Shorter working hours, restrictions on nightwork, extra time off for parents, more flexible working hours, the right to opt for part-time work yet keep open the chance of full-time work later, all these cost money. Capital has been able to accommodate recent demands for a basic week of 39 or 38 hours, but more radical steps will be more difficult.

Take for example the question of making hours more flexible. It is one thing to do this with office work. Beyond the investment in clocking-in equipment, it involves no extra cost and promises considerable gains. But try applying the same principle to factory work, where profits often depend on keeping the machines in continuous motion. If workers could choose their own time of arrival, the factory would need additional workers to cover the slack periods. Factories already take on more workers than they strictly need: they keep a pool of workers to cover for absenteeism and illness. With flexible working hours they would need an even larger back-up force.

Or think of the loss of output with a working week of 30 hours. So far, employers have covered shorter hours by sleight of hand. Workers get a shorter week, but lose some of their time for tea breaks and meal breaks. Or they get a shorter week, but have to speed up the work. As a result, wages have stayed largely intact despite the shorter week – employers have raised hourly rates to compensate for the loss of 1 or 2 hours' pay. How would these employers respond to a 30-hour week? No way of covering this by shorter tea breaks. In France, the move towards a 35-hour week by 1985 has meant lower wages: in most agreements, workers are only compensated up to about 60 per cent of the rate for the hours they lose. If the price for shorter hours is lower wages, what will British workers say to that? Or if the price for parental sick leave is higher taxes, what hope of achieving such reforms?

In a crisis, ambitious demands seem out of place. We see the national output shrinking, and feel the most we can do is distribute these diminishing rewards more fairly. None the less, we should press these demands. Any major shift in the sexual balance will have to mean sacrifices for men. When men have privileges, equality must mean they give these up. Taking work as a whole – waged work and domestic labour – men work fewer hours than women and get much more pay. Women are 40 per cent of the workforce, practically 100 per cent of the domestic workforce, but they end up with only 25 per cent of the pay. We cannot change this without taking from men and giving to women.

Looking on the brighter side, equality means redistribution, but it can be redistribution with much larger resources. Crisis always has two faces. It threatens what we used to take for granted, forcing us into unemployment, eroding the gains of previous years. At the same time it is a preface to revival, when capital lays the groundwork for its next phase of expansion. The building can be on capital's terms or it can be on ours. With a sufficiently powerful movement for shorter hours we can dictate terms that favour both women and workers as a whole.

Britain today is extraordinarily backward. It has antiquated machinery, managers whose only tactic is to increase the pace of work, an industrial base left over from years of imperial complacency. Add on to this the fact that so much of existing capacity is wasted through the crisis and we can see the scope for radical demands. With existing techniques and machinery, we could produce about 20 per cent more. With improved and modernised production, output could be even higher.

Left to themselves capitalists will take the easy way out. They will either flee the country (as they have already done in large numbers) or push down wages to levels that can compete with newly industrialising countries in the rest of the world. But we can refuse them these options. In the nineteenth century, the campaign for a 10-hour day forced capitalists as a whole out of the dead end (often literally) of lengthening the working day. It pushed them into making profits by raising productivity, instead of by keeping workers on the job for longer hours. Today, we can carry this process further. Employers complain of 'overmanning' – they want the easy option of carrying on as before but with fewer workers on the payroll. They will happily abdicate responsibility for modernising production. But if we refuse to comply with their conditions, they will have to turn their thoughts in a more progressive direction. We have to set new standards by which we are prepared to live.

British workers fall way behind in the league tables for the advanced capitalist countries – on both hours and wages we are behind most of Western Europe. We are told to compare ourselves with workers in the Philippines and count ourselves lucky with what we have. Why not set our sights higher? Why not compare ourselves with workers in Sweden, or indeed almost anywhere in Western Europe? There is no iron law of nature that dictates present conditions.

This does mean being tough with the owners and controllers of capital. They will always prefer the easy way out – why should they waste their efforts on meeting our demands? They will escape to happier climes if possible, looking for workers who are less insistent. One thing this means is tight controls against capital leaving the country; we have to find ways of closing the easy option. However, we must also face the possibility that capital will never co-operate; we must be prepared to take firms over when they sulk in the old conditions. The constraints we face are not particularly economic ones. Technically, we could have a good deal more than we get at the moment. The problems are political. This does not make them any easier to handle, but at least they are open to change.

Capitalism may be able to adjust itself to our demands. There have been times in the past when it seemed to have run out of steam, yet miraculously produced a new way forward. In the 1920s and 1930s millions were out of work, and many argued the only choice was socialism or barbarism. The rise of fascism seemed to confirm this assessment, but by the end of the second world war capitalism staged its comeback, offering growth and benefits for all.

It is hard to see what further magic is possible, what new tricks capitalism can pull out of its bag. But basically we have three options. We can accept the proposed cuts, adapt ourselves to even lower wages, fewer jobs, poorer social services, and give capitalism the easy way out. We can dig in our heels and demand more, leaving it up to capitalism to find a way of providing this. Or we can accept that capitalism is now past its prime and that the time has come for genuinely socialist, egalitarian policies.

Between the second and third it is hard to judge. If capitalism *can* guarantee us what we want, few will support the uncertainties of a socialist alternative. But if capitalism is unable to combine its own need for profit with our need for human existence, we have to look towards this alternative. The important thing is to say what we want, not tailor our demands to the meagre prospects of today. The old labourist demands – a job and a decent wage (in brackets read, for men) – are no longer enough. We want equality between men and women, and that means equal hours of labour at home and at work.

5.

The Family Wage

The idea that men are the breadwinners runs deep in our society. Whenever you suggest that women's jobs are as important as men's, or that men might do shorter hours at work and longer hours at home, this is the barrier you meet. Though everyone knows that women have jobs, few people take this seriously. The notion of man as breadwinner, woman as housekeeper still holds strong – despite mounting evidence against it. It matters more, people argue, that men have jobs because their wages support a wife and children; they are earning for the whole family.

This notion dates back to the nineteenth century. Early in that century men's wages were higher than women's, but no one rationalised this into a full-blown theory of the family wage. Men were not expected to earn enough to support dependants – on the contrary, all members of the family were pressed to look for work. Women and children were employed in large numbers in the new factories of the industrial revolution, and, for one brief moment, it looked as if capital might dispense with men altogether.

As the century wore on this trend was firmly halted. Factory Acts banned children from the mines and mills, making it necessary for one of the parents to stay home with them. Protective legislation removed women from jobs like mining, and new technology displaced them, often in favour of men. In middle-class circles the 'idle' wife appeared as proof of the family's prosperity. Lower down the scale the not-so-idle but at least non-working wife became the touchstone of working-class respectability. Skilled workers began to demand a family wage.

In the process the balance swung against working women. They retained their hold in textiles but made little headway in other industries. In the 1851 census one in four married women went out to work; by 1901 this was down to one in ten. For those women able to marry (and this, remember, was the century of the 'surplus women' when there were not enough husbands to go round) marriage usually meant an end to waged work. Families were large, and the total number of pregnancies even higher; married women were rarely capable of full-time employment. Going out to work became a male preserve, though women boosted the family income by taking in laundry, running a shop, or doing outwork for the many establishments that thrived on captive female labour.

More myth than reality

As feminists have pointed out, the family wage was more myth than reality. Only the higher-paid skilled workers earned enough to support an entire family, and in the 1911 census nearly one-third of family income was coming from other sources. In the majority of working-class households, the earnings of women and children were vital – 'idle' dependants were a rare luxury.

But, as myth, the family wage has powerful effects. Women were kept out of jobs – they did not, according to the argument, need them since they were supported by men. When women did go out to work they could be paid lower wages – after all, their earnings were just a supplement to family income. Trade unionists refused women entry to their unions, opposed their employment in better-paid jobs, and justified this discrimination by the argument that men had families to support. They campaigned against the employment of married women, bringing motions to the 1909 Labour Party and TUC conference that would have banned working wives.

Government commissions used the convention of the family wage to dismiss women's claim to equal pay, arguing in the aftermath of both world wars that women did not 'need' the wages paid to men. Men had families to support; women only themselves. For those women who had to work (and despite received opinion, very many supported not only themselves but their children, too) the assumptions of the family wage spelt acute hardship.

Today, when families are smaller and most married women go out to work, the mythology should be revealed as such. Male earnings now account for barely *half* household income, the rest coming from the earnings of women and children, or from state payments like child benefit. Only a tiny minority live under conditions sanctioned by the family wage: no more than 5 per cent of households fit the supposedly typical pattern of working man, non-working women, two dependent children.

Married or not, women do work, yet the fantasy of a family wage legitimises pitiful wages. Women in *full-time* work may get less than £60 a week, before deductions. We push this uncomfortable fact aside, saying they must be young girls living at home, or else married women supported by husbands. But what of the ones who are living on their own, or single mothers supporting their children? Nearly one million women now live as single parents, dependent on these 'women's wages', or surviving on a social security payment that will be stopped if they spend too much time with a man. We cannot go on pretending that women get extra financial support – too many have to live without it. And even when women do live with parents or husband, what excuse is this for low wages? Why should women depend on others for their keep?

In defence of the family wage?

When people defend the family wage they usually claim it pushes up wage levels. In 1982 the Trade Union Research Unit produced a paper *In Defence of the Family Wage*, finally taking up the cudgels on behalf of men. The paper begins with the extraordinary claim that 'there is nothing inherently sexist about the family wage' (it could be the woman who is breadwinner just as easily as the man!) and goes on to defend it as a weapon in wage negotiation. It means, the authors argue, that union negotiators can claim a minimum high enough to support two adults and two children, and so acts as a powerful weapon for the lower paid. Abandoning the family wage would weaken these workers, giving employers an excuse to pay less. We would find ourselves with minimum wages set by the needs of one individual – a minimum much lower than present poverty lines.

In her article 'Class struggle and the persistence of the working-class family', Jane Humphries has made similar points. She argues that in the nineteenth century the family wage meant gains for working-class families, with women sharing some of the benefits. Where workers established the family wage as a norm, she argues, they pushed up wage rates to compensate for the loss of the women's earnings. With only one wage-earner, the family got as good an income as it used to get from several. Women and children were released from their daily grind at the factory, and could use some of their free time to improve conditions at home. The hours gained from capital could be turned to cooking, sewing, growing vegetables, so that the same money income went further. Women's share of family income was less than men's, but even so they came out with more. Men got more from the change, but women benefited too.

As well as this, the argument goes, the family gave workers more strength in their battles with capital. If the family had disappeared – and so many nineteenth-century writers thought it might – the individual would have been exposed to the cruelties of the market. There would have been no protection for the young, the old, the sick, the unemployed. With a family-wage system it is possible to support non-working members of the family, saving them from the indignities of the workhouse. In the long run, women paid a tragic price for the introduction of the family wage, losing their claim to jobs in their own right. But in the short term, Jane Humphries argues, it meant gains for all.

But there is no firm evidence that keeping women out of work forced up wages for men. There is no proof that the family-wage model allowed for higher wages. On the contrary, we have plenty of evidence that men do *not* earn a family wage, plenty of evidence that women and children still have to seek jobs. If married women did not go out to work today, the numbers of households in poverty would quadruple. We know the family-wage model had not guaranteed high earnings for all men, so why do we assume it was responsible for the high earnings of any? If it has not prevented low wages, why do we act as if it caused high wages? The conditions that dictate wage levels are many and varied, and just because some male wages went up when the family wage entered the scene, we cannot conclude that the one was caused by the other.

What we *do* know is that the family-wage model has legitimated low wages for women, and justified the widely held belief that women should not take jobs when men are unemployed. The lowest-paid workers are women, and only the most miraculous of union negotiators could turn the family-wage argument to their advantage. For women living on their own, the model means poverty – and employers do not distinguish between single and married women when they make up the pay packets. For households where both man and woman work, the model means one and a half wages for two jobs.

The wages system as it operates today cannot cope with our real needs. Over a century and a half of union struggle and state regulation, a pattern has been woven that does not fit our lives. Young people are not supposed to need much (they are supported by their parents and have no children of their own) so they get low wages. Adult men are supposed to need more (they have the wife and children to support) so they can claim higher wages. Women are supposed to need nothing (they are supported by men) so they get the minimum necessary to persuade them to work.

When we step outside these stereotypes – when we have children too young, have more than two children, bring them up without the support of a father – we are plunged into poverty. Child benefit is too low to cover the full costs of bringing up a child, and wages too inflexible for our varied and changing needs.

Poor *and* dependent

Important as these arguments are, they are only one side of the picture. Sometimes the family wage is discussed as though it is a matter of poverty alone, as if the only issue is whether it guarantees us a living income. Does it make women richer or poorer? Did it raise or lower living standards? Is it a useful tool in wage negotiation? Does it keep families in poverty or wealth?

Setting it up like this implies that money is all that matters, that having enough to live on is the sum of human ambition. It makes the whole issue hang on the problem of poverty, as though the dependence of women is a minor quirk. It suggests we could put up with some people being dependants, as long as no one suffers material hardship – that it does not matter who earns the money, as long as there is enough to go round.

As feminists have always argued, the conventions of the family wage spell dependency for women. Their material needs may (if they are lucky) be met by the man's earnings – but they exist as kept women, dependent on the husband's good will. Those who doubt the importance of this should talk to the women who have gone back to work after years at home. However low their wages, it matters to them that they now have money of their own. Or they should talk to women who have left their men and find themselves for the first time entitled to claim supplementary benefit. However pathetic the payment, it is their own – no strings attached.

The way things are set up at the moment, women are forced into dependence on men, and the marriage that was once a choice can soon become a trap. A man who leaves his wife may well be better-off financially; a woman who leaves her husband finds herself saddled with the harsh realities of women's pay. As long as the wages system assumes some 'typical' family unit, it forces us into conformity – and for women this means conforming to the role of dependant.

One result is that women doubt their own right to work. In her book *Girls, Wives and Factory Lives*, Anna Pollert recounts her discussion with women in a Bristol tobacco factory. The women were quick to criticise the men in the factory and showed little reverence for male superiority. But when it came down to it, they wondered if they were entitled to work.

> Well, don't you think a man needs a job more? I think a married man needs a job more than we do.
>
> I don't really believe in married women working. Well, 'cos there's not much work anyway, and they ought to make room for people what've got to lead their own lives.

Of course they knew that few households could survive on male earnings, but the family-wage model put them on the defensive. They felt guilty that they might be taking work from men, though they realised very clearly that most men would refuse to do the jobs they did.

> I can't imagine a man doing my work. It's too boring for a man. Women have more patience.
>
> Men'd go mad. It'd kill them with boredom! Girls are expected to do that sort of thing. Girls are thought to be the weaker sex.

While everything conspires to keep women as dependants, they find it hard to challenge inequalities at work. It seems only fair that men should get the better-paid, more interesting jobs – after all, they have a family to support. When women go out to work, they sometimes feel they are lucky to get anything.

This ideology of the male breadwinner is extremely powerful, and one of the main blocks to women's equality. Again and again we hear the refrain: Why should women get jobs when men are out of work? Why should some households have two breadwinners when others have none? Trade unionists who say they support equality will draw back in a time of crisis. When the pressure is on, it is men's jobs, men's wages that always seem to matter most. We have to challenge this if we are to make any move in the direction of equality.

Sexism in tax and social security

The problem is not just an ideological one; it is built into the tax and social security system. Taxation in Britain takes it for granted that the man is the breadwinner. In recognition of his manly duties, the married man gets an extra tax bonus – the married man's tax allowance. First introduced in 1918, this has kept going through all the changes in women's employment, and now means nearly £6 a week extra to married men who pay taxes.

The tax benefits of marriage are paid to the man, and unless women make a special request for separate treatment, the tax returns will also be dealt with by him. A married woman's income is 'deemed for tax purposes to be his income and not to be her income', and until very recently tax offices refused to deal with married women. If a woman wrote in with a query, the reply would go to her husband. Nowadays, the system has conceded some points and women can opt to be taxed separately. But they can only do so if the husband first agrees – when it comes to taxation the man has the last word. The extent to which married women are subsumed under their husbands is illustrated by the fact that the Inland Revenue would need another 6,000 staff to cope with independent taxation for women.

If taxation is riddled with sexist assumptions, social security is definitely a man's world. The system treats men as heads of household and women figure in it mainly as dependants. Until recently, married women were encouraged to pay a reduced national insurance contribution. Those who took this option get no sickness or unemployment benefit. Those who paid the full stamp can claim for themselves, like any single woman or married man. But they cannot as yet claim for their children, except when the man is incapable of work.

The most oppressive edge of social security is the non-contributory side – supplementary benefits. At the time of writing, a married woman simply cannot claim. She is dependent on her man, and if he cannot provide for her he should put in a claim on her behalf. The system is so blatantly discriminatory that the government has been forced to amend it under EEC pressure. From 1983–4 it will be the 'main breadwinner' who can claim. If the married woman has been the household's main source of income for the previous 6 months, she will be able to claim for herself, husband and children. Note that the change clings fast to the principle that *someone* must be bread-winner – the only modification is that it allows for the occa-sional case where this is the woman.

It is because married women lose out so badly on social security that cohabitation has become an issue. A single woman (or separated or divorced) *can* claim supplementary benefit – but she will lose this right if she is deemed to be coha-biting with a man. The cohabitation rule justifies the worst kinds of social security 'snooping', and effectively means that women on their own should keep away from men. It trans-forms all emotional and sexual relations between men and women into ones where women are presumed to be 'kept' by a man in return for providing their services. But the real prob-lem is that married women get such a raw deal. If they got the same treatment as single women, the basis for cohabitation rules would disappear. If women were treated as people in their own right, instead of dependants on men, their sexual relationships would be nobody's business but their own.

Social security insists that men are breadwinners, women housekeepers. The two most blatant examples are the House-wives Non-Contributory Invalidity Pension and the Invalid Care Allowance. Married women cannot claim an allowance for looking after invalids, because this is assumed to be their normal job. If a man does it, he can claim an allowance; if a married woman does it, she will do it for free. Similarly, mar-ried women will not qualify for the invalidity pension if they are capable of doing housework. Men only have to prove they are incapable of going to work; women have to show they can-not do their 'normal' housework. The discrimination is stagger-ing, and indicates the power of the family-wage model. Women are treated as housewives not workers; they need no compensation when they cannot take a job.

Breaking out of dependency

The question is not only what is wrong with this, but how do we change it? Like many things it is a vicious circle: the more dependent you are, the greater your vulnerability to change. Women with young children need those male earnings, and women whose only alternative is low-paid boring work will welcome male support. The women most deeply trapped in relations of dependence are also the ones least able to challenge them. Any proposal that questions male responsibilities will seem like a threat. In her article 'The Family Wage', Hilary Land quotes a woman trade unionist as saying in 1911:

> Women with good cause dread anything which weakens the link between the breadwinner and his home . . . each of them knows perfectly well that the strength of her position in the home lies in the physical dependence of husband and children upon her.

The mechanisms of dependence are closely interlocked, and changing one without the others can leave women worse-off than before.

Take the question of divorce settlements. We can say that women should not be dependent on men, but does this mean they should get no maintenance? When they *are* financially disadvantaged, it seems perverse to deny them what little comfort the system has allowed. Or take the married man's tax allowance. We can say that this must be phased out in the interests of equality, with the extra resources perhaps used to raise all individual allowances. But what then of the women who depend on male incomes – women who earn nothing, or so little that a higher tax allowance will do them no good?

All this makes tax and social security a difficult area for reform. Feminists continue to debate the best solutions, and there is no simple 'feminist line'. Some see 'disaggregation' (that unwieldy term for basing tax and security benefits on individuals rather than on households) as the priority. If we want to break out of dependency we must alter the laws that justify

and confirm it. Others see the real problem in the lack of social
provision for young, sick and elderly, and argue that until we
have an alternative to the unpaid labour of housewives, dependency will remain. It is the familiar chicken-and-egg dilemma.
Tinkering with tax and social security may do little if all the
causes of dependence are left untouched. Leaving them as they
are only reinforces the assumptions that keep women down.

'Disaggregation' will not in itself end inequality, and whatever changes we support we have to keep this firmly in mind.
But tax and social security are under review: partly because the
EEC insists on a review of legislation that treats women differently; partly – and more ominously – because many Conservatives would like to see reforms that encourage women to stay
at home. We have to make our voices heard in this debate.

For example, some Conservatives now want to end the married man's tax allowance. Their objection is not that it favours
men over women. What they really dislike is that it favours
couples who both work over those where the wife stays at
home. A married man gets the allowance whatever his wife
does. The original justification was that he had to support a
non-working wife, but the allowance is not taken away if the
woman goes out to work.

The alternative proposed by some Conservatives is to abo-
lish the married man's allowance, substituting higher allowances for each individual. This may look more equal, but is in
fact designed to encourage women to stay at home. For the
crucial point in the proposal is that if the wife stays at home,
her allowance should be transferred to the husband. If he is the
sole breadwinner he could thus claim a double tax allowance;
if she goes out to work, he will drop back to a single one. No
more financial inducements for women to go out to work – if
anything, a pretty strong incentive for the husband to keep her
at home. Men and women would be technically equal, but all
the conventions of breadwinner and dependant would be
firmly reinstated.

The alternatives discussed by feminists are designed to challenge this breadwinner pattern. On tax and social security
there are *three* main proposals. First, we can abandon those

rules that treat us differently: end the married man's allowance; treat everyone as an individual for tax purposes; give women the same rights to invalidity pensions or invalid care allowances as men; allow unemployed women to claim for their dependent children and not just unemployed men. Second, we can raise child benefit to a realistic level – abolishing the married man's allowance could finance an extra £3 or £4 for each child, for a start. Third, we can allow anyone without a job – man or woman, married or unmarried – to claim supplementary benefit.

The first would give men and women formal equality. The second would challenge some of the rationale for paying men more than women. If the costs of having children were met through state benefits it would be harder to justify higher pay and better jobs for men. They could no longer say they have a family to support. The third would radically alter existing practices in social security: it would mean assessing our right to benefit only on our own income and no longer on that of our partners.

A woman without a job – as the feminist group Rights of Women puts it, 'whether the reason be lack of jobs, inadequate social services, intransigent menfolk, disability or whatever' – should be able to claim benefit. She might be living with a man who earns a good wage, but so what? We do not refuse people benefit because they have rich parents. If people have no income of their own they are entitled to one from the state. The partner's earnings should be irrelevant for men and women alike.

If such changes were introduced, marriage as a legal category would cease to exist. All of us would have the same rights and conditions – whether we live on our own, with partners of the same sex, the opposite sex, or in collective households. There would be no tax inducement encouraging people to marry, but no social security penalty if they succumb. It would be up to us how we chose to live our lives and not a concern of the state.

Replacing the family

Behind the family wage lurks the family, and in some ways we can only end the one when we replace the other. I do not mean that people should not be allowed to live in families – that children should be separated from parents or couples forced apart. But the family is still the main institution through which we care for the young, the sick and the elderly. As long as this is so, it is hard to break the breadwinner–dependant pattern.

At present, *someone* has to stay home to care for those in need. When children are young, most mothers stay home to look after them. When relatives are sick or disabled or too old to care for themselves, it is often the woman who steps in. Estimates suggest that *half* of all women can expect to spend part of their life caring for an elderly relative. If women cannot depend on male wages, how do we finance people to stay at home and do this work?

This remains the most controversial area in discussions of the family wage. Some feminists argue the answer is more socialised care – more nurseries, home helps, meals on wheels, special accommodation for the disabled and elderly, better old people's homes. Individual child care is not only a drain on the mother but a constraint for the child: it binds parent and child in an intense guilt-ridden relationship, limiting their capacity for being with others. As far as disabled and older people are concerned, they often prefer to keep their independence. If the services were available, they might choose to live on their own rather than with their daughters and sisters. Or if the facilities were better, they might prefer an old people's home.

But many will shrink from this alternative. Socialised care as we know it has little attraction: some people object to nurseries for their young children; many more object to packing old people off into homes. We have not given enough thought to the needs of the elderly and still lack a positive alternative to family care. We have given a lot of thought to the needs of children, but many mothers would still prefer to look after them at home.

No one wants to force children into nurseries, and no one wants to penalise those who choose to care for them at home. So the other alternative debated is a state benefit for those who care for people in need. The Labour Party, for example, has considered a 'home responsibility payment' – a cash allowance to anyone who has dependants at home. The tasks of caring for the young, sick and elderly would still be done in the home, but the people who did this work would be paid by the state instead of by their husbands.

The problem with this is that it so easily confirms women in their traditional role. Labour Party documents explicitly discuss the home responsibility payment as a payment to women – no one imagines the men as responsible. Everything at present points to the women. If their low wages did not make them the obvious choice, our stereotypes of the sexes would do the trick. Many feminists have rejected such solutions, as they rejected earlier proposals for 'wages for housework' paid by the state. It would still leave men and women grossly unequal – men going out to work and earning a wage, women staying at home with an inadequate state benefit.

For child care at least, one possible alternative would be an allowance for pre-school children, high enough to finance a nursery place, a childminder, or a parent at home. The advantage of this is that if offers us choice. If parents preferred to look after their children at home they could; if they preferred to use a nursery they could take this option. The disadvantage is that nurseries would then charge fees, which goes against what has been a long-standing demand in the women's movement.

The ideal solution is not obvious, but part of the problem is that we look at the issue in isolation. If we were making inroads into hours of work some of the dilemmas would dissolve. Men would be more free to take their share in caring for others; work would be less rigid and easier to combine with these other tasks. The hours strategy and the wages strategy go hand in hand.

Labour movement responses

How has the labour movement reacted to such debates? On
the face of it, socialists should welcome these proposals.
They question the vagaries of the wage system, pointing to a
future where income reflects need. At present we depend on
the chances of the job market, the accidents of trade union
strength, the lottery of marriage – it is pure fluke when our
income meets our needs. Sometimes we have more than
enough, sometimes we have too little. More likely than not,
it is when we have young children to support that we find
ourselves with least to live on. With a decent child benefit,
everyone (married or not) entitled to a living income, and
allowances for child care, could set off in a new direction.

In practice the labour movement has been rather lukewarm.
The issue of the family wage has been raised in recent TUC
discussions, and in 1980 the Tobacco Workers' Union made a
brave attempt to force the issue. It put this motion to the
annual conference:

> Congress believes that present policies on child and mater-
> nity benefits stem from an outdated concept of a 'family
> wage'. Congress therefore calls for a complete review of
> existing schemes to provide for substantial increases in
> family benefits.

The motion was remitted after the minimum of speeches
(one!) and later passed to the TUC committee on social insurance and industrial welfare. It has since been treated as an
appeal for higher child benefit, with its wider implications lost.

When feminists have proposed changes to tax and social
security, trade unionists have discovered endless problems –
some real, but some just capitulation to male privilege. Some
of the issues are like those that were raised when child tax
allowance (paid to the father) was abolished in favour of child
benefit (paid to the mother). How will the men feel if their
married man's tax allowance is taken away? How will they feel
when their pay packet shrinks, and the only compensation is

higher child benefit and possibly unemployment pay for their non-working wives? The answer has to be: they may not like it, but this is no excuse.

Despite such rumblings, the labour movement *has* adapted itself to phasing out the married man's allowance (a proposal on which there is now wide consensus) and using the resources to raise child benefit. But this is the easier part of the package – who would oppose higher child benefit? The really difficult one to win is the proposal that married women claim supplementary benefit in their own right.

Many in the Labour Party have rejected this out of hand – as too expensive, and also, they claim, too unfair. They argue it would unduly favour wealthy households; they shudder at the idea of a millionaire's wife collecting her weekly benefit. But this is no argument. Our tax system certainly needs rethinking – at present, it does little to redistribute wealth from rich to poor. But then we should turn our attention to this, instead of relying on the happy convention that men share their wealth with their wives. Equal benefits to everyone without work, financed by a genuinely progressive system of taxation, would be much fairer than what we have now. There should be no problem in ensuring that the increase in the millionaire's tax bill is higher than the benefit paid to his wife!

When people argue against 'disaggregation' what they really mean is that women's dependence is a side-issue. 'Nothing wrong with things at present. Too many complications in making a change. Why not leave things as they are?' The arguments are familiar ones, and echo those used against the earlier campaign for family allowances.

Then, as now, the issue was the family wage. In the 1920s Eleanor Rathbone argued that family allowances could save women from dependency and low pay. Wages, she argued, should cover just the needs of the workers. There should be a cash allowance to cover the costs of feeding and clothing each child, and a mother's allowance (like a home responsibility payment) for those who stayed at home to look after their children. As she put it in her book *The Disinherited Family*, 'a man has no right to keep half the world in purgatory because he enjoys playing redeemer to his own wife and children'. The needs of children and mothers should be met by the state, not depend on male generosity. The demands of children should not be played off against women's right to work and equal pay.

Then, as now, feminists divided on the issue, some fearing that cash allowances would pay women to stay at home. Then, as now, many in the labour movement rejected the proposals, fearing they would weaken wage negotiations and force down wages to individual subsistence levels. In 1930 the TUC refused to support family allowances, calling instead for better social services – an alternative that would have been more convincing if the TUC had campaigned for them. Ramsay Macdonald denounced family allowances as an 'insane outburst of individualism' – women and children were, he believed, quite adequately cared for by their men. Only the Independent Labour Party supported the demand, embracing it as part of an ambitious programme for raising workers' incomes and redistributing from those with money to those in need. The Labour Party was unconvinced. Not until 1941 did it grudgingly admit that cash allowances for children might not 'materially handicap the unions in their present fight to maintain and improve living standards'.

These anxieties have little basis today, when most wage bargaining is about relativities or keeping up with inflation. The only unions who still use the family-wage model to support their claims are those who represent low-paid workers: here, the level of social security payment for two adults and two children is sometimes employed to set the target for pay. But most of the low-paid workers are women, and a family-wage model carries little conviction for them. Employers can claim their female employees are dependants rather than breadwinners, and set the wages with this in mind. The family wage is not a vital, or even a useful model for wage claims. It is a dangerous argument for women.

The only serious issue is whether we want women more dependent on the state. If women escape from male patronage into the unloving arms of the state, is this a victory? If we break the breadwinner–dependant pattern, but replace it with dependence on state benefits, is this what we desire?

This question comes up every time the family wage is under attack. The arguments from the 1920s now seem like scare-mongering. Would family allowances 'eliminate' the husband? Would they lead to the 'nationalisation of married women and children'? Arguments today make a more sober point. We see state benefits eroded year by year. Can we really trust the capitalist state to provide adequate payments for children and non-working women? With all the humiliations of dependency, would women not be better off depending on male wages?

To some extent the question is misplaced. If women were paid for all the things they now do for free, there would be more incentive to do things differently. If, for example, mothers were paid when they look after their children, the real costs of their labour would appear for the first time. Building a nursery would no longer be a luxury, but a social saving. Or if women were paid when they care for the sick, shutting down hospitals would become too costly. And if married women were paid when they had no job, their unemployment would be counted at last. The pressures to create work would be that much stronger. So when feminists call for benefits for women, they are not saying women should live off such benefits; in the long run, these changes would mean fewer women at home.

When it comes to child benefit there *is* a problem, and anyone who has traced the sorry history of the maternity grant (stuck at £25 since 1967, which at today's values would be £120) can see the dangers in relying on the state. But what alternative is there? Wages have never been a satisfactory solution because they do not adjust to the numbers of children in each household. People do not have the regulation number – some have none, and some have four or five. Taxes are no better: if we rely on tax allowances to compensate parents for the extra cost of their children, this is unfair on those with lower incomes. If they are below the tax threshold, they get no compensation. Cash benefits to cover the costs of feeding and clothing the children, combined with cash allowances to cover their care, seem the best way forward.

Inevitably, this means more demands on the state, and

maintaining or improving provision will be a continuous struggle. But rather than shy away from this into the non-solution of present-day wages, we should extend trade union bargaining to cover such benefits. It is heartening that in recent years the unions have treated benefits as their concern, with the TUC pressing for continual improvements. Once we admit that the family wage has failed both women and children, we have to push this further, demanding more and better benefits from the state.

This does mean a shift in union priorities, away from localised bargaining over individual wage levels, towards more centralised demands over national benefits. The labour movement is as yet unconvinced about the dangers of the family wage – will it prove a useful ally? Even on the (widely agreed) need for higher child benefits, trade unionists speak with a muted voice. When it comes to women's claim for an independent income, they respond with stony silence. The relationship between feminism and trade unionism is a difficult one, and it is to this I turn in the final chapter.

6.

Between the Devil and the Deep Blue Sea: Unions and the State

Trade unions are still male organisations. In the nineteenth century, the craft unions carefully excluded women. In the twentieth century, trade unionists have made it clear that they want no competition from women workers. After the first world war, and in the mounting unemployment of the 1920s and 1930s, unions repeatedly called for a ban on working women. Again and again, they passed motions condemning the employment of married women, sometimes, it seemed, the employment of any women at all. The tramworkers resolved in 1919 that women must go; local government workers decided in 1935 that married women must go; the railwayworkers declared in 1937 their 'grave concern' with the employment of women as clerks. These examples were not unusual, and as late as 1947 the TUC annual report declared that 'It would be doing a grave injury to the life of the nation if women were persuaded or forced to neglect their domestic duties in order to enter industry.'

Today, one in three trade unionists is a woman, but how many do we see at union conferences? Women do not get elected to the General Council – the few women members there are almost always elected to the reserved women's seats. Women are rarely appointed as union officials, and few get on to union executives. In the public image, trade unionism is a masculine affair, and though women appear on the picket lines and in the demonstrations, it is men who speak for them on TV.

Some unions are predictably male: mining is by law a man's

job and the railways by tradition a male enclave, so no one expects them to have a female executive. But what of the Transport and General Workers' Union? Nearly one in five of its members is a woman, yet it has an all male executive and a heavily male image. Or what of the General Municipal, Boilermakers and Allied Trades Union? One in three members is a woman, but there is only *one* woman on the executive. And what of those unions who represent the nurses, the teachers, librarians, bank clerks? Typically female workers, typically represented by men.

None of this is static and there have been major changes. In the union with the largest contingent of women workers – the National Union of Public Employees – positive action has opened up the lower levels of union activity and secured women a voice on the higher committees. As far as national policy goes, the TUC now has its own charter for women at work, for the under-fives, for positive action in the unions – all influenced by the women's movement and setting impressive goals.

Union business has been extensively redefined to include issues once dismissed as irrelevant. In 1979 the TUC staged its first national demonstration in defence of the Abortion Act, thereby admitting that abortion rights are a union concern. Local government workers have initiated campaigns around sexual harassment at work, something that many trade unionists would once have seen as a non-issue. Women involved in these campaigns still get a hostile response – the old cry of 'What has this to do with unions?' – or the sexual banter that substitutes for serious discussion. But abortion and sexual harassment are increasingly admitted as union business, and for better or worse the official seal of approval still goes a long way. 'If it's union policy, I suppose we have to listen.'

These *are* changes and they testify to years of stuggle by women trade unionists. Yet on many issues union practice works against women. Unions are formally committed to equal pay, but they fight their battles in the name of differentials, clambering up a league table that rests on inequality. Unions are formally committed to women's right of work, but some still call for a family wage that could support a woman in dependence. Unions express concern about low pay, but few support the campaign for a minimum wage. Unions say they want shorter hours but cannot agree a policy of statutory limits. The labour movement has its own way of doing things and has been slow to adjust to the demands of women.

Free collective bargaining

Free collective bargaining has been the great god of British trade unionism. Union membership is higher in Britain than in other European countries and legislation over pay and conditions is more frowned upon. Local negotiation by shop stewards is still at the heart of union practice, and many trade unionists have been uneasy over the trend towards centralised bargaining. When it comes to interference by the state, they are often downright hostile.

As far as pay is concerned, national agreements may set the basic wage, but for many male workers the pay packet depends on locally negotiated shift premiums, overtime rates, or productivity bonuses. The result is that pay and conditions vary even within the same industry and trade, but unions have defended this as a source of strength. The classic argument is that localised struggle forces up standards for all. The better organised blaze the trail, clearing a path for those who follow.

The history of pay increases largely bears out this defence. But it is a vanguardist vision, where the 'shock troops' are sent in to breach capital's defences, pulling the others in their wake. Engineering workers at Metal Box negotiate a 35-hour week; engineering workers elswhere can build on this to further their own claims. The miners go on strike for higher pay; less powerful workers can set their targets by the miners' gains. Or, as Cynthia Cockburn has put it in her book *Brothers*, pay bargaining can be like 'dancing a conga' – 'the leaders prance on, pulling behind them in a snake of diminishing earnings the less-skilled or less-organised groups of workers'.

Faced with a powerful shop steward network, management has often favoured more centralised negotiation. In British

Leyland, piecework has been largely replaced by measured daywork, and management paid a high price for the change-over. Piecework rates were determined job by job, giving a boost to local strength; measured daywork centralises the bargaining at a level management can cope with. Correctly or not, British Leyland equated centralised negotiation with weaker trade unions – and it is an equation that many workers also make.

One consequence is that unions are suspicious of the law, preferring to advance their interests on their own terrain. Legislation to secure the rights of trade unionists is one thing; legislation as a *substitute* for collective action is quite another. Up till the last moment, for example, unions doubted the importance of legislation for equal pay. Way back in the 1880s the TUC passed its first motion in support of equal pay, but then sat back and left it to the 'established procedures' and 'voluntary methods'. Predictably enough, nothing happened, and women's wages continued to hover around 60 per cent of men's. In 1963 came the breakthrough, and the TUC passed a motion committing it to campaign for an equal pay law. Yet as late as 1969, when Barbara Castle unveiled plans for an Equal Pay Act, the General Council of the TUC was still talking about its time-honoured voluntary methods, with perhaps a smattering of legislation to deal with really obnoxious employers. The traditions of free collective bargaining scorn the use of the law, and trade unionists see it as proof of weakness when they turn to its aid.

The women's movement has also kept its distance from the law, arguing that our strength comes from ourselves and not from legislation. Few feminists built their hopes on an Equal Pay Act and many reject the state as a patriarchal institution. But when it comes to conditions at work it is not enough to rely on local strength. Women homeworkers have little hope of union power and where homeworkers *have* organised in a union branch, it has often been because they were workers who used to be employed as full-timers for the company. For instance, glove makers in Devon set up a branch of the General and Municipal Workers' Union in 1975, and rapidly won major increases in pay. But here it helped that the factories they worked for were already unionised *and* that many of the homeworkers had previously done jobs in the factory. Without this link, unionisation would have been far more difficult.

Part-time workers are similarly handicapped, and many find they have neither the time nor the money to get involved in unions. Full-time women workers may be in small firms or family shops, with little hope of building a union. Others work in the public sector, in jobs that have none of the bargaining power we associate with miners or dockers. For such women, legal sanctions can be a powerful weapon. Yet many trade unionists continue to deride their role.

Today, the main argument is over a statutory minimum wage. Within the TUC the National Union of Public Employees has fought a lonely battle for this demand, with powerful opposition from some of the big guns in the movement like the Transport and General Workers' Union. The labour movement has agreed a target for low-paid workers – two-thirds the average male wage, which at the time of writing is about £90 – but prefers to stick to its usual methods in meeting this target. The arguments are predictable. How can unions objects to wage control if they say they want a statutory minimum? If some workers are pushed up to a statutory minimum, will this not pull other workers down? If the state takes over from the unions, what hope is there of getting low-paid workers to join a union?

Some of the arguments are pure traditionalism, fuelled by the contempt of the strong for those who have failed to make their way. There is only one real point. Trade unionists fear that state regulation can undermine their vitality, reducing them to a paper membership. Active membership can dwindle when there is nothing left to do. As any branch offficial will confirm, people do not turn up to meetings when all the decisions are taken elsewhere. The more we leave to the state, the argument goes, the less we will do ourselves. Trade unions could decline into paper tigers.

It is an argument for leaving things as they are, but think

what that means for low-paid workers. On the TUC's own definition of low pay, there are currently seven million workers earning less than a minimum wage. The gap between high-paid and low-paid workers has stayed much the same for over a century – what does free collective bargaining offer to those at the bottom of the pile? It is all very well to say they should organise, but for many workers the cards are stacked against them. Some, like the health workers, *have* organised – but their pay is still abysmally low.

The differentials game

Free collective bargaining makes defending differentials a crucial part of the game. Workers may have few illusions about the league table – they know as well as anyone that their place depends on might rather than right. But it is a game, they argue, in which everyone can win. One group presses ahead, another comes in behind saying we must restore differentials. Each jostles to maintain its place in line and in the process money wages are continually raised.

This is fine as long as we accept the hierarchy, but for lower-paid workers it means the old familiar place at the end of the queue. Better-paid workers may express sympathy, but they have no intention of bridging the gap. For women, this kind of trade unionism is no solution. They have not slipped down the league table – they have always been in another division. Decades of collective bargaining did little to raise their pay and it took a deeply flawed Equal Pay Act to make any difference. Free collective bargaining as currently practised offers little hope for change.

In 1978, Beatrix Campbell and Valerie Charlton launched an attack on labour movement traditions in their polemic 'Work to rule'. It was the end of years of incomes policies, when wages had been restrained and differentials squeezed. The 'social contract' had lost whatever credibility it once had (remember those slogans about the 'social con-trick'?) and most socialists looked forward to a return to free collective bargaining. 'Work to rule' sounded a more sceptical note.

What, it asked, will the wages offensive do for equal pay?
How can the survival-of-the-fittest strategy help those at the
bottom of the pile? Wages militancy will only consolidate differentials, give most to those who have, and little to others. It
will take for granted the conventions of the family wage, and
divert attention from the monumental task of achieving sexual
equality. 'In our opinion,' the authors concluded, 'free collective bargaining is not an effective socialist economic strategy
against capitalism, nor is it in any way a strategy for women's
equality.'

Two years later, when free collective bargaining was firmly
re-established, Beatrix Campbell returned to the fray with
'United we fall'. She argued against differentials (the 'sacred
cow' of the labour movement) and for flat-rate increases. She
argued against the excessive reliance on shift premiums, overtime rates, productivity bonuses, and for a wage policy based
on the basic wage. Trade unionism, she said, must get itself out
of its rut, or it 'will be left loitering without intent in the pre-
history of modern capitalism, a muscle-bound Tarzan, a man
of few words wielding blunt instruments'. We must seek an
alternative to this primitive vision, and the ones she proposed
are those discussed at length in this book: shorter working
hours; a new relationship between waged work and child care;
an end to the family wage. We must turn away from the jungle
morality, towards an egalitarian resolution at a 'national political level'.

This takes us into deep water. Equality for women means a
major shift in priorities and a revolution in the nature of work.
The problem with unions is not just that they are male-dominated. They are also parochial. They operate trade by trade,
workplace by workplace, seemingly incapable of a broader
approach. They are used to looking for more of the same, and
are at a loss when we ask for something different. If we want
to challenge the differentials game and introduce new criteria
of sexual equality, we must, it is argued, look for another ally.
The argument leads us towards the state.

A feminist incomes policy?

One possible conclusion of this approach is that women need a feminist incomes policy. State regulation of wages could be egalitarian in a way that free collective bargaining never can. Whatever we think about incomes policies, at least some of those imposed in the 1970s adopted the principle of a flat-rate increase. In 1975, for example, the government introduced a maximum rise of £6 a week, with no rise at all for those in the £8,500 plus bracket. Over these years of wage control there was a convergence in average pay, with low-paid women workers edging up towards the higher-paid men. When incomes policies were abandoned in the late 1970s, women's pay fell behind again. Perhaps we should learn from this experience, as Beatrix Campbell suggests, and put our weight behind a feminist incomes policy?

It is a deeply iconoclastic argument. Socialists traditionally oppose incomes policies, seeing them as little more than a cover for cutting wages. Supporters of the alternative economic strategy have been classified as 'right' or 'left' depending on their attitude to wage control. Yet here come these women, claiming – in the name of an even greater radicalism – that incomes policies can be progressive. What are we to make of this?

If it were just a matter of past incomes policies we could reject the argument. As Angela Weir and Mary McIntosh demonstrate in their article 'Towards a wages strategy for women', it was the Equal Pay Act that pushed up women's wages, not incomes policies. The incomes policies of the 1970s paid lip-service to the poor, but made no efforts to secure improvements. The 1974 social contract set a minimum pay target of £30 a week – and what happened? In those worst-paid industries where wages are set by a Wage Council, most rates were still under £30 nearly two years later. The 1975 policy set a £6 maximum, but made no attempt to ensure that the lowest-paid got this maximum. If employers could get away with less – and employers of low-paid workers were often best placed for this – they did so. Incomes policies used the plight of the low-paid to condemn the free-for-all of the wages offensive. Tested against the results, they showed little real concern. The policy was one of restraint, and redistribution was just the democratic veneer.

With this experience behind us, why should we expect any better in the future? Why expect the state to be more progressive than the labour movement? The state has been no friend to women. As Angela Weir and Mary McIntosh put it:

> Rights for women have had a very low priority in state policy. The post-war welfare state was constructed on lines which both reinforce and reproduce traditional sexual divisions of labour with the family. All government policy is excluded from the Sex Discrimination Act. The Equal Pay Act contains probably one of the most restrictive definitions of equal pay which does not even comply with EEC requirements. Maternity rights and benefits are among the poorest in Europe.

The state is no alternative to the unions; the one is no less patriarchal than the other. We cannot turn to incomes policies as a reliable weapon for equality. On past experience they are not so progressive.

The debate over incomes policy – and here I mean not just the debate among feminists but the parallel debates among socialists – draws on the confusions of today's mixed economy. If we all worked for private employers and the government came along with a pay policy, we would recognise it immediately for what it was. Our sacrifices would be to someone else's advantage. If at the other extreme we worked under a system of social ownership, with popular involvement in planning decisions, then planning income would be as sensible as planning anything else. 'Should we take a rise this year or invest our surplus in new hospitals?' If it was 'our' surplus we could ask such questions, though we would certainly disagree on the answers.

Britain today fits neither extreme. Incomes policies mean workers take less so employers can get more. But when so many of us work for the state we can be persuaded that our sacrifice is financing better schools, more hospitals. We can certainly see that when some workers strike others suffer. Under these conditions an incomes policy looks more plausible: it does take from workers to give to capital, but it also takes from some workers to give to others. And faced with today's inequalities, many still support incomes policies as a fairer system of distribution.

My own argument against incomes policies is simply that we cannot trust the state. Incomes policies have used the rhetoric of equality to disguise a reality of cuts. Trade unionists were persuaded in the 1960s and 1970s that it was in their interests, and then found themselves with no guarantees. We could argue that if the unions struck a harder bargain we might find ourselves with something in return. But then, as Angela Weir and Mary McIntosh point out, 'after abusing trade unions for their male chauvinism, their complicity through collective bargaining in holding down women's pay, it seems odd to be dependent on those very same unions in negotiating a new strategic incomes policy.' Incomes policies would only favour women if the labour movement had been won to the cause of sexual equality. But if it *had* been won over, the feminist case for an incomes policy would fall. The real task is changing the unions themselves.

Getting out of the rut

Trade unionism must, as Beatrix Campbell argues, get out of its rut. It should aim at equality rather than hierarchy. It should attack both low pay and differentials.

Today's differentials are often arbitrary, products of a long and complex history. There is no neat correspondence between what you earn and what you do; differentials do not reflect the length of training, level of skill, attractions of the work. All these may contribute, but when the overwhelming pattern is low wages for women and high wages for men, we have to suspect something more. Take the large Scottish teaching hospital whose basic rates for 1983 are set out in the recent TUC book

Working Women (see Figure 1). The shaded areas indicate the jobs done by women. And these are just the basic rates. If we added in overtime and bonuses, this would push up earnings for the porters and drivers, making an even sharper contrast between men and women workers.

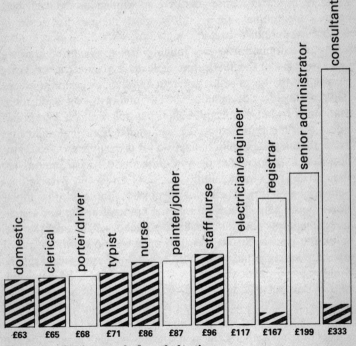

Figure 1   **Basic rates before deductions**

We have to rethink these hierarchies, give up the differentials game, commit ourselves to ending low pay. And we have to recognise that this means redistributing income. When Barbara Castle introduced equal pay legislation, she shocked the labour movement by declaring that the easiest way to equal pay for women would be if the men agreed to stand still. But is it not more shocking that seven million workers get less than what the TUC considers a minimum wage? Or that in the same hospital some workers earn £63 a week and others £333?

It is not enough to raise women's wages; we have to make them equal to men's. As long as women earn so much less than men they will be treated as marginal to the labour force. They will be expected to give up *their* jobs when the children are young; they will depend on male earnings for any of the luxuries of life. If women are to catch up with men, the men will have to stand still.

When differentials are so deeply entrenched this may sound like pure utopianism. But equality has a powerful appeal. Governments in the 1970s and 1980s have played on our sympathies for the lower-paid, and much of the pay restraint of the 1970s was sold in their name. Trade unionists conceded their chances of higher pay in the belief that this would favour those worse-off than themselves. I have argued that they miscalculated, that incomes policies have so far done little for the poor. But what matters is that people *did* support redistribution – it was and is a popular demand.

There was a time when unions spoke for those with nothing, when they fought their battles in the name of justice and equality. Now they are derided as the agents of injustice: trade union barons who wield their power in their own selfish interests, condemning the weaker to fall behind. It is an exaggerated picture if only because it overstates so much the power of the unions. But as long as the unions cling to differentials, such accusations have a ring of truth. If the unions are to keep their legitimacy they must speak again for equality.

This means changing the pattern of wage claims – instituting an 'incomes policy' for the labour movement itself, imposed from below instead of above. We need massive increases for the lower-paid, smaller increases for the higher-paid, and a ceiling, I believe, for the highest of all. We need, as Beatrix Campbell has said, flat-rate increases instead of percentage ones, a steady erosion of the gaps between us. And we need one major piece of state intervention – a legally binding minimum wage.

Attacking low pay

The problem of low pay is getting worse. If we take the two-thirds average male earnings as a goal, the number of people on low incomes has increased in recent years. In 1979 less than one male manual worker in ten was low paid, but by 1982 this had gone up to nearly one in six. In 1979 two out of three manual women workers were low paid, but by 1982 this had gone up to three in four. These figures spell misery for millions of workers, yet the solution is easily within our grasp. In their article 'Ending low pay', Liz Bisset and Stuart Weir estimate that raising all wages to two-thirds average male earnings would only add 3 to 5 per cent to the total wage bill.

Such increases are possible, but will not happen without legal sanctions. In France there has been a statutory minimum wage since 1950. This was dramatically raised as a result of workers' action in 1968, and by the late 1970s stood at nearly two-thirds average industrial earnings. In the Netherlands a statutory minimum wage was introduced in the second world war, and by the late 1970s this stood at three-quarters average manual earnings in manufacturing. In Norway a statutory minimum was introduced in 1980, which states that average manual earnings in each company must reach at least 85 per cent of the national average. In Belgium, where nearly three-quarters of the labour force is unionised, unions nevertheless fought hard for the introduction of a statutory minimum and won their demand in 1975.

In Britain, the Labour Party and TUC have begun to consider the demand more seriously, but neither has so far moved into action. The most they will commit themselves to is discussion – an advance, certainly, on earlier years, but not one that takes us much further. The traditions of free collective bargaining still stand in the way.

Trade unionists have argued that a legal minimum wage is a substitute for union strength, pointing to the example of France, where less than one in four workers is in a union. They conveniently forget the other European countries, where large and powerful labour movements have insisted on minimum wage legislation. Trade unionists have pointed to the failures of the wage council system, which sets minimum wages for nearly three million workers in catering, hairdressing, laundry work,

clothing manufacture, etc. They have used the appallingly low
wages for these industries as an argument *against* a legal minimum, instead of using the figures to call for a higher rate. They
have suggested that such workers would be better served by
joining a union, ignoring the evidence that when wage councils
are abolished, the low wages continue.

It is a kind of megalomania which claims that the union will
be the answer to everything, forgetting that for many workers
a union is a distant dream. Free collective bargaining does not
work for all. We must face this fact, without, of course, deny-
ing the very real fear that trade unionists have of state regulation. Instead of turning their backs on a minimum wage, trade
unionists should look at how they can use such legislation to
build up their strength. What role can they play in implement-
ing it? Should they provide the inspectors, instead of the state?

Beyond these arguments, the only serious question is
whether a statutory minimum would squeeze workers out of
jobs. Would it not force some of the smaller firms into liquida-
tion, making things even worse for their workers? As the Low
Pay Unit has pointed out, this argument implies that all
employers already pay the maximum they can afford to their
workers, that wages already reflect the productivity of the
workers. Yet when employers are in a position of strength, it
is more than likely that they get away with murder. Certainly,
a legal minimum would have to be carefully introduced and the
employment effects carefully monitored. One suggestion is
that the state could help employers who prove they are in trou-
ble by reducing their National Insurance contributions.
Another suggestion is that national and local governments
could set up co-operatives or other publicly accountable enter-
prises in the sectors where capital is most weak. There *are*
problems, but none of them so overwhelming as the problems
faced by workers on poverty wages.

Unions or the state?

To summarise, the choice is never unions *or* the state. There
are certain changes which can only occur through state action.

Only central government can finance the massive improvement we need in child care. As the women's movement has consistently argued, community *control* of nurseries is crucial, but equal provision for all parts of the country means *funding* at a national level. Disaggregation of tax and social security clearly implies demands on the state, since it is the state which operates the system.

The touchy areas are those where legislation interferes in what used to be a union concern – legislation over overtime, to limit nightwork, to set a legal minimum for pay. The argument here – and unions accepted this when it came to legislation on health and safety at work – is that a progressive law can strengthen us in our demands. It can set minimum conditions for all and a framework in which we can mobilise for maximum ones. Legislation here is not a substitute for union strength but an aid to it. Where the problem is the employers, trade unions could well use the support of the law.

Where the problem is the unions themselves, it is unlikely that the state can help. As long as unions oppose a fairer distribution of income, we will not get an egalitarian incomes policy. There might be some point in the future where such incomes policies could work, where the majority of trade unionists have been won over to equality, but some pockets of resistance remain. But we have a long way to go before we reach that point. The first task is winning the unions. There is no short cut to equality, bypassing the vested interests of the labour movement, appealing over its head to a benign state.

This is not to say that women should put all their eggs into one basket, working exclusively inside the unions. We know there are other ways to organise. The National Abortion Campaign has fought successive attempts to limit abortion rights, without much help from the labour movement until the 1979 campaign against the Corrie Bill. Women have organised widely against male violence against women, and trade union campaigns over sexual harassment are only a minor spin-off from this. The National Child Care Campaign draws on unions and community groups alike. The campaign for a statutory minimum wage could well develop outside the TUC.

The unions are not the panacea that their leaders sometimes pretend, but they are a source of popular power. As Jenny Beale has said in *Getting It Together*, 'women will carry on fighting for what they want with or without trade unions. But there is little doubt that a union is the best vehicle for achieving change at work.' The negative side is simply that the unions *are* a bastion of male power, with male dominance writ large. Precisely because of this, women have to take them on.

The issue is not unions *or* the state, and, to put it more broadly, the issue is not policy *or* struggle. The language of policy has its own seductions. We can all too easily convince ourselves that if we find the 'right' policy, the rest will follow. This benefit structure or that? These working hours or some other? It can sound absurdly complacent, as if we are already in position of power and casting around for things to do. Our energies can go on refining the details, with little left over for winning support.

Perhaps the early 1980s bred such complacency. The Labour Party was in flux and open to change. In constituency after constituency, new voices were heard and new issues raised. A few extra clauses and the world would be ours. Today, the mood is more realistic. At a local level there are councils working towards an alternative – in Greater London, Sheffield, the West Midlands – but their powers are limited and under constant threat. At a national level it is hard to feel great optimism. There will be no miracle from the top down, no battle won in committee rooms alone. We face a long and arduous struggle for a better life and formulating policy is only part of that struggle.

Change will come when people are convinced – when they know what they want and can see it is possible. This is why policies are so important. The last few years have been rich in new proposals and feminists and socialists have been spelling out what they want. Maybe this *was* based on delusion, a false belief in imminent change. But it gives us a lasting legacy for political action. It helps us translate the dreams into reality, and develop a vision for the future that meets with the here and now.

The future is female

On a world scale, the economy is increasingly female. In the newly industrialising countries of South-East Asia, it is women who fill the factories, producing textiles, computer components and electronic gadgets for the world. In Britain the full-time housewife is dying out and a new working class being born. Men have been thrown out of the older industries like coal, steel and ship-building. Women have been brought into the expanding service sector and the new industries in electronics and computers. It is a time of crisis, when the industries that used to provide men with their strength are threatened, and the jobs they used to claim as their own are destroyed. Many find themselves dependent on their wives' earnings, both challenged and supported by women at work. Some respond by calling on women to return to the home and clear a space for the more needy men. Others admit that times have changed and that we must build our future on a new foundation.

We have to recognise that this *is* a moment of crisis, when the old traditions are up for question. Many industries are in flux, and the print workers, described in Cynthia Cockburn's book *Brothers*, are facing the kind of changes that others will recognise. In this industry, as elsewhere, technology is shaking up the old hierarchies, exposing a new and uncomfortable similarity between printer and typist: 'Computerised composition has hit the compositor's craft a terrible blow, shaking the class and gender relations that have been developing over centuries, throwing them into a maelstrom of confusion.' It is a time of upheaval, from which printers might advance or else retreat. As Cynthia Cockburn predicts:

> Men are likely to respond in one of two ways: by hitting back, reasserting sexual primacy with whatever means are at hand; or by accepting the dismantling of male power in favour of a more egalitarian way of living and organising.

Male dominance has too long a history for easy optimism, but with everything in turmoil, new hopes arise.

This is why we must go beyond today's strategies. As currently discussed, economic strategy encourages us to go on as before. It turns political questions into technical matters; it focuses on the means and forgets the ends. Think of those interminable debates on how to raise investment, whether to introduce import controls, how to control the city. Important as these are, they divert us from the essential question: What is it that we want? By avoiding this question, the debates imply that we already know – which can only mean recycling those well-worn demands of yesterday. We need something better.

Despite the delusions of some Tory politicians (remember Patrick Jenkin with his 'If the good Lord had intended us all having equal rights to go out to work and to behave equally, you know he really wouldn't have created us man and woman'?), women workers are here to stay. They have re-entered the man's world of work and brought with them new questions. Why do we have to restore differentials, when differentials mean inequality? Why are men entitled to a family wage, when women are also slaving away? Why do women walk a tightrope between their children and their jobs, when men are parents, too? Why do women end up with the double shift, while men enjoy the comforts of home? We cannot answer these questions with the old slogans. They point towards a new strategy, based on different working hours, genuine equality of pay, and social provision for the young, old and infirm.

No one pretends this will be easy. The dead weight of tradition presses hard and is reinforced by the vested interests of men. Women's inequality is all too often to men's advantage, promising them the better jobs, the higher pay, and someone to care for them when they get home from work. There are only fleeting moments of alliance. Women want shorter hours to change conditions in the home; men want shorter hours to create more jobs. Women need a better system of child support to free them from dependency; men need a better system to rescue them from overtime. Women are fed up with low pay; men know that low-paid women could threaten their own jobs. Women are demanding a better world for themselves;

men want a better world for their daughters. There are moments when the interests of the sexes converge, but in all these moments there are tensions pulling us apart. The conflicts between the sexes are real, and genuine gains for women mean losses for men. Unity is a long-term goal.

The important thing is not to be crushed by the crisis. As unemployment rises and cuts go deeper we are all too ready to retreat, abandoning our wilder aspirations for another day. It seems hard enough to defend what we have, utopian to insist on more. But a crisis always has two faces, and while one of them sternly bids us put up with what we have, the other looks forward to the future. The old ways are under threat. Instead of rallying to their defence we should set new terms for a better world. Equality should be our goal and the strategies we devise should work to this end.

A Guide to Reading

Chapter 1

For a quick survey of conditions for women there is a useful report on *Women in the Eighties* (Counter Information Services 1981). For conditions and issues, see *Working Women* (TUC 1983). For something more detailed see *Women at Work* by Lindsay Mackie and Polly Patullo (Tavistock 1977). Jenny Hurstfield has done a comprehensive account of women as part-time workers in *The Part-Time Trap* (Low Pay Unit 1978). For conditions and issues, see *Working Women* (TUC 1983). For the most up-to-date study of home-workers, see the pamphlet by Liz Bisset and Ursula Huws, (to be published by the Low Pay Unit in 1983). Ann Oakley's *Housewife* (Allen Lane 1974) is good on the experience of being a housewife; Hilary Land's article 'Who cares for the family?' (*Journal on Social Policy*, vol. 7 no. 3 1978), shows how government policy presumes on women doing unpaid work at home.

Three recent articles in *Marxism Today* pick up on the changing shape of the British economy, and discuss the growing importance of women in the labour force. These are Gwyn Williams' 'Land of our fathers' (August 1982), which discusses the changes in Wales; Anne Showstack Sassoon's 'Dual role: women and Britain's crisis' (December 1982); and Doreen Massey's 'The shape of things to come' (April 1983), which looks at the way firms have moved to different parts of the country.

Chapter 2

For a good defence of the alternative economic strategy, have a look at the CSE London Working Group's *The Alternative Economic Strategy* (CSE Books and the Labour Co-ordinating Committee 1980), or Sam Aaronovitch's *The Road from Thatcherism* (Lawrence & Wishart 1981). Both are written from the more radical side of the strategy. Ian Gough's *The Political Economy of the Welfare State* (Macmillan 1979) helps explain the post-war development and crisis of the welfare state, and David Hall's *The Cuts Machine* (Pluto Press 1983) demonstrates the lop-sided accounting that makes public services always seem a cost.

There are numerous feminist critiques of the AES, mainly in journals like *New Socialist* or *Marxism Today*. The most challenging is Anna Coote's 'The AES: a new starting point' (*New Socialist*, no. 2 1981), which questions the fundamental assumptions, and suggests we start from the problem of caring for children rather than the problem of growth. The most detailed feminist critique is Jean Gardiner and Sheila Smith's 'Feminism and the alternative economic strategy' in *Socialist Economic Review 1982* (Merlin Press 1982). In the same issue of *Socialist Economic Review* is an interesting discussion of the weight we place on manufacturing: Henry Neuburger's 'Does manufacturing deserve special status?'

Chapter 3

The NCCL Rights for Women Unit is a good source for policy proposals on women. See particularly the excellent book *Positive Action For Women – The Next Step*, written by Sadie Robarts, with Anna Coote and Elizabeth Ball (NCCL 1981); and Ann Sedley's pamphlet *Part-Time Workers Need Full-Time Rights* (NCCL 1980). Mandy Snell discusses the failings of present legislation in her article 'The Equal Pay and Sex Discrimination Acts: their impact in the workplace' (*Feminist Review*, no. 1 1979).

The idea that women want more than the right to work,

more even than equality with men, is widely shared within the women's movement. As far as the issues raised in this book are concerned, a crucial contribution was Beatrix Campbell and Valerie Charlton's 'Work to rule', and later Beatrix Campbell's 'United we fall'. These were published in the socialist feminist paper *Red Rag* in 1978 and 1980 and cover in the space of a few pages virtually all the issues raised in this book. 'Work to rule' has been reprinted in the Feminist Anthology Collective's *No Turning Back* (The Women's Press 1981), and the ideas of both articles are summarised in Beatrix Campbell's 'Women: not what they bargained for' (*Marxism Today*, March 1982).

Chapter 4

Rudolf Bahro's *The Alternative in Eastern Europe* (New Left Books 1978), is an exciting discussion of changing work, particularly in part three of the book. André Gorz's *Farewell to the Working Class* (Pluto Press 1982) is more idiosyncratic and loosely argued, but also takes up the issues of work and time.

The TUC produces regular reports on its *Campaign for Reduced Working Time*, which give details on recent union agreements and information on the hours worked in Britain and elsewhere. The Department of Employment produces an annual *New Earnings Survey*, which gives details on both earnings and hours. The Department has also printed a paper by Michael White on 'Shorter working time through national industry agreements' (*Department of Employment Research Paper 38*, September 1982), which discusses the effects on employers of the 39-hour week for engineering and construction. The Anglo-German Foundation for the Study of Industrial Society has published reports on *Working Time in Britain* and *Working Time in West Germany*, both in 1981. These are virtually unreadable, but do try to assess the impact of shorter hours on jobs and output.

New Ways to Work (currently funded by the Greater London Council) is an organisation which exists to promote job-sharing and can be contacted at 347a Upper Street, London N1

0PD. Its publications include an attack on the government policy of job-splitting, *Job-Sharing v Job-Splitting* (1983).

Chapter 5

Fran Bennett has written an excellent survey of current policy proposals on the family wage, outlining the debates between feminists: 'The state, welfare and women's indepedence' in *What Is To Be Done About The Family?*, edited by Lynne Segal (Penguin 1983). Other articles in this book are also relevant, as is Michele Barrett and Mary McIntosh's *The Antisocial Family* (Verso Editions 1982).

Jane Humphries writes about the rise of the family-wage system in 'Class struggle and the persistence of the working-class family' (*Cambridge Journal of Economics*, vol.1, no.3 1977). Michele Barrett and Mary McIntosh criticise this in 'The "family wage": some problems for socialists and feminists (*Capital and Class*, no. 11 1980). The Trade Union Research Unit at Ruskin College published 'In defence of the family wage' (*Occasional Paper 72*, 1982).

Hilary Land has written various excellent pieces on the family-wage system and its effects. Her article 'The family wage' (*Feminist Review*, no. 6 1980) is particularly interesting for its discussion of the earlier campaigns around family allowances, led by Eleanor Rathbone. Ann Pollert's *Girls, Wives and Factory Lives* (Macmillan 1981), captures some of the contradictory consequences of a breadwinner ideology, when it is combined with women's experience of going out to work.

Chapter 6

Two useful introductions to the role of women within trade unions are Anna Coote and Peter Kellner's *Hear This, Brother – Women Workers and Union Power* (New Statesman 1980), and Jenny Beale's *Getting It Together* (Pluto Press 1982). Sarah Boston's *Women Workers and the Trade Unions* (Davis-Poynter 1980), traces the historical relationship.

For tracking down Beatrix Campbell's writings, check under

the guide to reading for Chapter 4. Angela Weir and Mary McIntosh have criticised her idea of a feminist incomes policy in their article 'Towards a wages strategy for women' (*Feminist Review*, no. 10 1982).

The Low Pay Unit is a good source of information on all aspects of low pay, and has been active in pressing for a minimum wage. It can be contacted at 9 Poland Street, London W1V 3DG. Specifically on the minimum wage there is the pamphlet the Unit produced in 1983, *The Case for a Minimum Wage*, written by Chris Pond and Steve Winyard, and a useful article by Liz Bisset and Stuart Weir, 'Ending low pay' (*New Socialist*, no. 11 1983).

Brothers by Cynthia Cockburn (Pluto Press 1983), is a fascinating account of the way craft workers in the print industry have used their control of technology to keep women out, and a challenging analysis of the possibilities opened up by today's technological change.

Jenny Beale
Getting It Together

'I already do two jobs – I'm a worker and a mother. Now you are saying I should do three jobs and be a shop steward as well.' (June, APEX).

Many things – from sexism to domestic ties to the restrictions of part-time work – hold women back from involvement in trade unions. But when women do join, they enrich trade unionism, bringing strong traditions of action and a powerful challenge to traditional priorities.

Getting It Together examines the overlap between feminist politics and trade unionism and shows that housework and childcare should concern all trade unionists.

Jenny Beale has been a tutor in trade union education and feminist politics for many years. She has written articles on health and safety and many aspects of trades union education.

£2.50   ISBN 0 86104 500 9

David Hall
The cuts machine

While health, housing and education are reeling from round after round of public spending cuts, the Tory government has increased public borrowing to lend £4 billion to private companies.

The Cuts Machine shows how public services are controlled in secret and subordinated to the interests of private business. The national accounts, the tax system, the operation of government borrowing, the controls on spending and the controls on workers all operate on the assumption that public services produce nothing of value.

The limitations of Labour Party and TUC alternative economic strategies are exposed. David Hall argues that a political strategy must rise out of the fights for jobs, services and democratic controls.

David Hall was until recently research officer for the Society of Civil and Public Servants. He now works for the Labour Research Department and writes regularly on public spending.

£2.50   ISBN 0-86104-504-1

Bob Sutcliffe
Hard times

More people are unemployed today than ever before. The miracles of the post-war boom are forgotten and production stagnates. Governments everywhere are cutting already inadequate welfare services.

Hard Times shows how this economic nightmare has resulted from the capitalist system's need for profit and how government policies will impose yet more hardship worldwide. It criticises existing alternative plans and argues for a more radical, democratic and internationalist approach.

Bob Sutcliffe teaches economics at Kingston Polytechnic. He is co-author, with Andrew Glyn, of **British Capitalism, Workers and the Profits Squeeze.**

£2.50   ISBN 0-86104-505-X